Theosophy
Simplified

Cover art by

Jane A. Evans

Theosophy Simplified

by Irving S. Cooper

*This publication made possible
with the assistance of the Kern Foundation*

The Theosophical Publishing House
Wheaton, Ill. U. S. A.
Madras, India / London, England

First published in 1915

Second Quest Edition, 1989

Library of Congress Catalog Number: 78-64905
ISBN Number: 0-8365-0651-1

Printed in the United States of America

To
C. W. L.
who first showed me the Light

CONTENTS

PREFACE TO THE SECOND EDITION

This introduction to Theosophy is as clear and useful as it was when it first came out in 1915. The text has been lightly edited to conform with modern usage, one or two short passages on science rewritten and updated, and the suggestions for further reading added. The text still reflects the clarity of its author's understanding.

—Ed

AUTHOR'S PREFACE

This simple outline of the teachings of Theosophy is intended for those who are commencing their study of the subject, and to be of service to teachers of classes in elementary Theosophy. Its only recommendation is its simplicity and directness of statement, to attain which no effort has been spared.

INTRODUCTION

Perhaps your first thought on seeing a title such as *Theosophy Simplified* is that it is so watered-down, so diluted that the real meaning of "Theosophy" is altogether lost. But if you take into consideration that you must learn arithmetic before higher mathematics or basic grammar and sentence structure before undertaking to write a book, you will see that it is not necessarily a bad thing.

For one to want to learn a little, in general, before launching into a deep, scholarly study of a subject is logical, even commendable. It was customary when I was a child for my father to ask the farmer to "plug" a watermelon before he bought it. By this he meant for the seller to take a sharp knife and cut a deep tapering plug from the melon to see if it was ripe and red deep inside. No one objected to taking this sample cut. We took the melon home and plunged deeply into it—*if* it first stood up to my father's scrutiny. And so it is in this case, too, I think, that before you enroll in an advanced class to study the inner meanings, the Sanskrit words and their possible translation, the implications of certain obtuse statements, isn't it best to know the basic premises?

It is generally understood that Helena Petrovna Blavatsky, one of the principal founders of the Theosophical Society, was an extremely brilliant woman, well-educated, a gifted linguist, and a finely developed clairvoyant who was able to work under the tutelage of the Masters. It is only to be expected that her writings are evidence of the highest scholarship, but it is also historically true that, in the beginning, such works as *Isis Unveiled* and her masterpiece, *The Secret Doctrine*, were intended to appeal only to the intelligentsia. There had been no plan to couch the ancient sacred teachings in the vernacular of the person on the street or disseminate it abroad to the masses.

The early journals, published by Theosophists were aimed primarily at the well educated to interest them in this admittedly difficult study and to promote exchanges between those scholarly readers as they delved into the Ancient Wisdom. More difficult, too, because as HPB told them, *all* of the teachings, *all* of the explanations could not then be given out.

Hard on the heels of the first publication of *The Secret Doctrine*, students and followers began dialogues with each other as well as with the founders to try to fathom the tremendous amount of esoteric material in this huge work. It was not an easy task to read, to study. You can only partly imagine the understanding and intellect it took to write it! HPB never sidestepped the issue of her works being difficult to grasp. In *Lucifer*, Vol. VI, No. 34 (London, June 15, 1890), she answered a letter on this very subject, saying:

> If my work is, at this day of materialistic assumptions and universal iconoclasm, too premature for the masses of the profane—so much the worse for the masses. But it was not too premature for the earnest students of theosophy—except those, perhaps, who had hoped that a treatise on such intricate correspondences as exist between the religions and philosophies of the almost forgotten Past, and those of the modern day, could be as simple as a shilling "shocker" from a railway stall.*

---

*In the terms of the late 1800s, this would be comparable to a "penny dreadful," a "dime novel" or to today's mass market paperbacks.

Even one system of philosophy at a time, whether that
of Kant or of Herbert Spencer, of Spinoza or of Hart-
mann, requires more than a study of several years.
Does it not, therefore, stand to reason that a work
which compares several dozens of philosophies and over
a half-a-dozen of world religions, a work which has to
unveil the roots with the greatest precautions, as it can
only *hint* at the secret blossoms here and there—cannot
be comprehended at a first reading, nor even after several, unless the reader elaborates for himself a system
for it?

The intellectual exercise of tracking down an obscure
usage or a classical reference was more common in
those days than it is today. Today, when education is
more widely accessible to more people, we find that
the mental pursuits are more likely to be the reading of
condensations or predigested study notes from which
to write a report. Many a self-proclaimed New Age
seeker of today demands that his or her "Path" be "en-
gineered with all the selfish craft of modern comfort,
macadamized, laid out with swift railways and tele-
graphs, and even telescopes, through which he may,
while sitting at his ease, survey the works of other people; and while criticizing them, look out for the easiest,
in order to play at the Occultist and Amateur Student
of Theosophy." This statement was written not in *New
Age Journal*, not in *New Realities*, *East-West Journal*,
or *Alternatives*, but by HPB in 1890.

She went on to say that "the real 'Path' to esoteric
knowledge is very different. Its entrance is overgrown
with brambles of neglect, the travesties of truth during
long ages block the way, and it is obscured by the
proud contempt of self-sufficiency and every verity distorted out of all focus."

One of the first facts that a student must compre-
hend is that the Wisdom Teachings have been passed
down through unimaginable eons of time. They come

to us from earlier races, from fragments found in the earliest known writings, from the *Vedas,* and from early Egyptian lore which tells us that it was already ancient when it appeared in Egypt, from the *Stanzas of Dzyan* and even earlier oral traditions passed along to students and disciples in ages before—far, far before the beginning of written history of this present age. Though this may be difficult for the uninitiated to understand, try to grasp that all of these many and varied sources agree on the basic teachings.

An illustration is a children's game that perhaps you played, in which a group sits in a circle. The first one whispers something to the one seated to his left, and she in turn whispers it to one sitting on her left, and so on and so on until the circle has been completed. There are roars of laughter when the last person repeats the words aloud as she heard them, and they all then hear what the original sentence was when it began. With a circle of only ten or twelve people, a short sentence can change unrecognizably.

Think for a moment what countless ages and countless persons these teachings have passed through. The fact that the hidden wisdom has remained seems a miracle. Only, there *are* no miracles; there are fundamental laws and fundamental facts that remain new, unchanged, basic. These facts have come down to us in many languages in many ceremonies in many guises, but the underlying truths, once unveiled of their surface symbols, are there—starkly pure.

One of the most familiar uses of symbols is the alphabet. Each letter has an individual sound, its representation. To build a word we must know the individual symbols, the letters. From words we can then build sentences that express ideas or designate things. To bridge the gap between our own experiences and the metaphysical, we need simple analogies which can be easily grasped. We do not want to learn anything which will have to be *changed* later on, but only what will be the same basic truth, no matter how compounded it may become. In *The Ancient Wisdom* Annie Besant, a leading theosophical teacher, wrote:

> An elementary textbook cannot pretend to give the fullness of knowledge that may be obtained from abstruser works, but it should leave the student with clear fundamental ideas on the subject, with much indeed to add by future study but with little to unlearn.

It is like trying to read and figure out words without first learning the alphabet; you realize that those basic elements are essential. You know that they will never have to be "unlearned." Alfred Taylor, in his *Commentaries and Analogies, Series I,* said, "The esoteric approach to spiritual truths is through correspondences and analogies." A basic study of a subject must use your own simple knowledge on which to build more difficult concepts and more complicated explanations.

What are these first fundamental ideas? Annie Besant said:

> It is admitted on all hands that a survey of the great religions of the world shows that they hold in common many religious, ethical, and philosophical ideas. But while the fact is universally granted, the explanation of the fact is a matter of dispute.

Through the study of the Ancient Wisdom you can learn the common ancestry of all the world's great religions, and doing this can promote understanding and a conscious striving to further our evolutionary process. It is well worth the application of our wills and our minds. That first step—the decision to study—is like striking a single note on a piano: you hear it ring true and learn that note's sound. And step by step you learn to press down other keys simultaneously to build a beautiful, harmonic chord. But you also learn that the whole is greater than its parts. So it is with the study of Theosophy.

Esoteric or occult wisdom is underlying the structure of religion past and present, simply because it is the *truth*. The founders of the Theosophical Society, HPB and Col. Henry Olcott, were visiting the Maharaja of Benares in December 1880 when they learned of his family's motto—*There is no Religion higher than Truth*— and, with the Maharaja's permission, adopted it as the motto of the Society. Olcott immediately began using it in the journal *The Theosophist*. Truth, in esoteric or exoteric studies, remains what it *is*. The value of a number, for example 8, remains the same even if you designate it as A/Y in an algebraic equation. The value of a fact—the truth—remains the same regardless of how it is expressed, whatever words may be used, in whatever analogy it is described, in whatever symbol it is shown. Mere descriptive words cannot change it.

Before you decide to take a course in a subject, you must have some idea as to what the subject is. The study of French entails learning the language spoken in France—simple. The study of semantics is the study of the meaning and derivation of words, but it *can* go into an area somewhat like logic or general semantics, and surprisingly, logic involves mathematical procedures! From this second illustration you can readily see that it is not always so simple to arrive at what a study is all about. Many want to know just what Theosophy is, and I think that cofounder William Quan Judge said it beautifully:

Theosophy, meaning knowledge of or about God—not in the sense of a personal anthropomorphic God, but in that of divine "godly" wisdom—includes the whole of both the known and the unknown. It follows that "Theosophy" must imply wisdom respecting the absolute, and since the absolute is without beginning and eternal, then it also implies that this wisdom must have existed always.

The study of Theosophy, or Theo-sophia, can be very simply outlined, made as basic as a child's lessons in Sunday school: it remains for the trained mind to go deeply into a theological study to become a minister or priest. So it is with any subject you wish to pursue. You must begin somewhere—at a point at which understanding can take place. As you digest more, you can take in more and more facts, each piece of information a building block which can support the complicated structure of an intricate philosophy. The building blocks of Theosophy can be stated simply. As understanding develops, upon deeper and deeper study, the student is able to flesh out the original skeletal information first received and come to recognize what may be called "the body of knowledge." Again I quote Judge, who wrote in his *Epitome of Theosophical Teachings:*

> There being of necessity various grades among students of this wisdom-religion, it stands to reason that those belonging to the lower degrees are able to give out only so much of the knowledge as is the appanage of the grade they have reached, and depend, to some extent, for further information upon students who are higher yet.

And yet there are those who have devoted an entire lifetime to such study only to be confounded by the realization of how little they *know*.

It is common to meet people who have only been introduced to the teachings, after a few short months or a few brief years of study, who state that they *know* the teachings. Those who have dedicated their minds and their hearts to unraveling the elusive threads which make up the embroidery constituting the whole design of the ageless wisdom feel only inept that they know so little of the whole. These latter face the simple truth that it is the slow, steady advancement through many lifetimes that marks the passage of the disciple. They try very hard to clear themselves of the clutter of personality and hope to be better prepared for acceptance in the next incarnation—or the next.

To paraphrase, even the longest journey begins with the first step. In this instance those first steps are the underlying principles of the esoteric study, the basic bricks with which you can build the highest edifice. But without those basic building blocks which are the foundation, the structure is nothing. The design of the universe is built of the most basic forms, yet with them it weaves the unimaginable glory which it is. One should never disdain those simple underpinnings; they are the bedrock of all that follows.

As a prima ballerina of widest renown still begins each day with the simplest exercises, so those who consider themselves advanced can hardly go wrong by referring to the fundamental truths underlying the profound wisdom. It is hoped that the word "simple" is not equated with something not worthy of note, but rather that it will transmit the feeling of being unadorned. In A. P. Sinnett's *Man's Place in the Universe* (1902), he said:

> . . . the vastness of extent and complexity in detail in even of the fragments we have been privileged to receive, are a bar to the absolutely simple statement

which a handbook is supposed to constitute. . . . The main outlines of the subject which have been specially brought before Western students may indeed be summed up so shortly that a child might understand them. . . . But simplicity and lucidity shall be our aim, the most transcendent heights of thought have to be faced at the very first step.

Here then is presented the unadorned basics of Theosophy by Irving S. Cooper who was an excellent and concise writer of these wonderful facts, the alphabet of esoteric wisdom from which all the words are built.

R. S.

1

THE SOURCES AND NATURE
OF THEOSOPHY

*Theosophy is, then, the archaic Wisdom-Religion,
the esoteric doctrine once known in every ancient
country having claims to civilization. This "Wisdom" all the old writings show is an emanation of
the divine Principle; and the clear comprehension
of it is typified in such names as the Indian Budh,
the Babylonian Nebo, the Thoth of Memphis, The
Hermes of Greece; . . . and finally the Vedas,
from the word "to know".*

*H. P. Blavatsky,
A Modern Panarion*

1

THE SOURCES AND NATURE OF THEOSOPHY

TWO SOURCES

When an unfamiliar system of thought is presented for consideration, it is always legitimate to ask, "What are the sources of your information?" Our willingness to take the time and expend the energy necessary to study that system naturally depends upon the clearness and reasonableness of the answer. So in presenting the teachings of Theosophy it is right to expect that a frank statement be made as to the sources of theosophical knowledge.

These sources are of two kinds:

(1) Those which are accessible at once to any thoughtful person with normal intellectual capacities, and

(2) Those which may be reached only after preliminary training and development of the character, mind and subtle senses.

An objection may be made to the second kind, by one commencing the study of Theosophy, on the ground that all information obtained in this way must be taken—at least for a time—on the statements of others. This is of course true, yet we are accustomed constantly to adopt this attitude. In fact, the greater part of current knowledge cannot be verified by the ordinary untrained person, but is accepted solely on the statements of experts.

For example, we read and believe many statements about atoms, yet none of us, without long scientific training, could duplicate the experiments by which these statements are proved. We accept the conclusions of astronomers regarding the movements of the sun, moon and stars, even though these conclusions contradict the evidence of our senses, because we have faith in those who have made a specialty of astronomy. Musicians tell us of the superb technical mastery of Liszt, and we believe them, though it would take us years of painstaking study and practice before we could realize this for ourselves.

It is not unreasonable, therefore, in commencing the study of Theosophy to accept as *possible* the statements made by experts trained in theosophical investigation. Later, if it is thought worthwhile, an effort may be made to verify these statements and convince ourselves of the truth of the deeper teachings of Theosophy. Of course, it is unwise to accept a statement as a truth merely because it is made by another person, but it is also equally unwise to deny it until we actually know the facts. The best course is to hold to the middle path and neither deny nor affirm, but to empty the mind of prejudice and preconceived notions and submit everything to the criterion of the reasoning consciousness of the intuition.

GREAT RELIGIONS

The first of these sources, which are accessible at once to a thoughtful person, is the teaching of the great religions of the world. When we begin the study of comparative religion, we seem lost in a maze of contradictions and even of absurdities, but with practice we become able in thought to strip away the ceremonials, forms and customs peculiar to each religion and get at the fundamental ideas and teachings common to all.

The differences which exist between one religion and another are due to the various characteristics of the people who hold them and to the deposit of ceremonies, speculations and fancies which, during the centuries, has gradually obscured or covered up the basic truths taught by their founders. Fundamentally, all religions are one, for sympathetic study clearly indicates that they teach the same core of truth and inculcate the same ideals of conduct and life.

In their externals, however, religions are unlike each other, for the reason that they were *planned* to appeal to different races and temperaments. At our existing stage of growth, one religion cannot and does not satisfy the religious needs of the whole world, for generally, when it comes to religious matters, we are more influenced by the way we are taught than by the teachings themselves. The mental and emotional characteristics of each race determine the most suitable form of instruction and, as these characteristics vary, so each religion differs in its externals in order to produce the desired result. "As fits each separate human need, so seems My Image," beautifully suggests God's attitude to humans.

It takes a certain bigness of mind to study sympathetically each religion for the truth it contains, since it is necessary to eliminate undue partiality for one form of worship, to learn to think in terms and symbols of each faith studied, to overcome prejudice, to practice tolerance and to be a lover of truth. But if this can be done by the student, *the basic teachings underlying all the great religions will be found to be perfectly in accord with the teachings of Theosophy.* This is why Theosophy appeals to the followers of every religion and explains why Christians and Buddhists, Hindus and Parsees, Hebrews and Muhammadans, though still retaining their religion, have joined the Theosophical Society. They all find in Theosophy that which illuminates their own religious beliefs and aids them to live the higher life inculcated by their scriptures. This is also the reason why Theosophy does not emphasize the superiority of one religion over all others, for each great faith has its message to the world, and humanity would be poorer without it. While Theosophy is not a religion—since its teachings are unaccompanied by ritual or ceremonial—nevertheless it is profoundly religious, as it teaches the essential truths found in all religions.

ANCIENT MYSTERIES

A great many theosophical truths may be found in studying the fragments of the instruction given in the ancient Mysteries which have come down to us. These famous institutions, which flourished in Persia, Egypt, Greece and Rome, were founded for the purpose of giving to the advanced people of the time a philosophical and rational interpretation of the myths and legends, which satisfied the common people and constituted the popular religions. Though only scattered portions of the once secret teachings now remain, still the attentive student is rewarded by occasionally finding a precious truth half-hidden in the obscure phrases of these old instructions.

PHILOSOPHICAL SCHOOLS

Another more fruitful field of study is found in the teachings of several philosophic schools which rose to power and fell to obscurity during earlier centuries. The wonder Pythagorean discipline of Crotona; the brilliant Neoplatonic Schools of Alexandria, particularly that which centered around Hypatia; the much misunderstood alchemists, whose symbology tinged the writings of the Middle Ages; the interesting Rosicrucian Orders, the undercurrent of whose teachings permeated the whole of European thought during the fifteenth, sixteenth and seventeenth centuries; and the Masonic movement which followed; all those are sources of theosophic knowledge. The statements made in the ancient books and rare manuscripts in which this information may be found are usually difficult to understand because they are expressed in quaint symbols and obsolete phrases, but persistent study is richly rewarded.

SCIENCE

Modern Theosophy is greatly indebted to science for its discoveries and for the exact terminology which has resulted from the careful manner in which the statements of scientists have been formulated. Modern Theosophy is equally careful in its methods of research, and its phraseology has gradually become more precise.

Theosophists of ancient and medieval times were often vague and obscure when they attempted to describe what they saw or to formulate the laws governing human growth and existence. This was due, not to any effort on their part to describe things which did not exist, but to the immensity of their conceptions concerning God and the universe, or perhaps they felt these to be too profound to be profaned by words. That is why symbolism was so largely employed then but is to a great extent unnecessary now. The richly descriptive language of science has taken the place of the symbol. How could early investigators describe electricity, an atom, a vibration, the planes of nature, when the terms themselves had not been coined and even the most cultured people knew nothing of such things? How could they explain clearly the evolution of the human soul by means of repeated lives on earth when the evolution of human bodies had not yet been thought of? Thus the modern presentation of Theosophy, which is decidedly scientific in tone and treatment, was made possible only because of the development of science.

The teachings of Theosophy include those of science, and every *proved* result of scientific research finds its place in Theosophy. In certain cases theosophical investigators, using special methods of research, have anticipated science, and scientists have later verified in their own way the results thus obtained. In still other instances Theosophy has carried the application of certain laws governing matter beyond the limits arbitrarily set by scientists, but this was justified because observation has shown that a *principle of repetition* prevails everywhere, and that nature repeats, in miniature in the physical world, processes that are universal in their scope.

INCOMPLETE KNOWLEDGE

The study of religions and ancient schools of philosophic thought combined with a knowledge of scientific discoveries is *not* sufficient, however, to explain satisfactorily all the conditions and phenomena of the world. Serious gaps still remain in our mental scheme of things; we seem unable to reconcile certain apparent conflicting viewpoints; and above all we need a guiding clue to lead us through the maze of speculations to truth itself.

As examples of conflicting viewpoints, we need only compare the statements of religion with those of science. The religionist speaks of God as the source and creator of all things; the scientist declares that the universe was formed through the agency of various forces obeying mechanical laws. The religionist tells of God's love for all creatures; the scientist points to the undeserved misery and suffering of humans, even babies, and the mute agony of thousands of animals and birds. The religionist considers the life beyond the grave, the scientist turns to a dead body and asks for proof that there is anything other than that. The religionist accepts ancient books as final authority; the scientist refuses to admit anything to be true except that which can be verified now. These antagonisms are doubtless due to *incomplete* knowledge, but how can that knowledge be gained which will show that religion, science, philosophy and art are but different aspects of the same body of truth? Is it not obvious that, if this world is a unity, such a synthesis must exist?

This leads us to the consideration of those sources of theosophic knowledge which require preliminary training and development of the character, mind and subtle senses before they may be reached.

PSYCHIC INVESTIGATION

Theosophy has never agreed with the dogmatic declaration of materialists that there is nothing superphysical, or of agnostics, that superphysical things might exist but we could never know them because of the limitations of the senses, though it has always emphasized that *there is nothing supernatural,* everything taking place within the domain of natural law. Theosophy has affirmed, upon the basis of actual experience, that there are inactive senses in every human being which, when stimulated to activity, would make possible the investigation of a normally unseen realm of nonphysical matter around us.

Instead of using physical instruments, however, which naturally have serious limitations, even though most delicately constructed, theosophical investigators in their researches have made use of the much more difficult method of developing within themselves the power to see this realm without the mediation of any instrument. Long and arduous training is necessary before this can be done, and it is made exceptionally difficult because one's character must also be acceptable.

A scientist may be sensual, cruel and selfish, but his scientific work will not be impaired if his intellectual and observational powers are keen. Those, however, who wish to take up the theosophical method of investigation must first refine and ennoble their characters. In so doing, they not only hasten the awakening of those subtle senses by means of which they come in touch with the unseen world, but also eliminate the possibility of misuse of those psychic faculties after awakening them—a serious thing.

There are a few people who have had the courage to commence and the patience to persevere with this severe training and have, after years of labor, become expert in this ancient method of investigation. Modern Theosophy is heavily indebted to them for the information thus obtained, for their published researches have raised Theosophy from the level of a speculative philosophy to the position of a world power in the domain of thought, because of its richness of detail and exactitude of statement. And what they have done, others can do—provided there is willingness to pay the price of constant effort, unselfish labor and the capacity to learn through failure.

The results of the investigations of these experts are priceless, if we attempt to estimate their value to humanity. These researchers have discovered many interesting and important things regarding the etheric part of the physical world and the invisible spheres—invisible, that is, to the normal human eye—which surround and envelop the earth. They have published a wealth of detail concerning the conditions which exist on the other side of death, the nature and appearance of the emotional, mental and soul bodies, the laws of human growth and of destiny, the purpose of existence and the swiftest way to reach the goal of human evolution.

Much of the exact detail which distinguishes modern Theosophy from all other schools of thinking along similar lines is due to the labors of these experts, who have spent years in obtaining the facts published and in verifying by repeated experiments and observations the conclusions to which they have come.

THE MASTERS

There is still one more source, the greatest of all, from which Theosophy has derived its most important information, and that is certain perfected beings, called sometimes the Brothers and sometimes the Masters, who have completed their human evolution but remain in touch with the world to assist humanity in its growth. They are distinguished by fully awakened subtle senses, superb intellect and lofty spirituality, and have at their command a vast knowledge of nature's laws, which is the fruit of age-long experience. They place this knowledge at the disposal of aspirants under certain conditions, generally that those who ask for it shall do so not by mere words, but by the noble, unselfish life they lead, dedicated to the service of humanity.

The information which the Masters have given to those who have thus qualified themselves to receive it has rounded out and completed the theosophical system of thought in a most wonderful way and has filled in many gaps in our knowledge. Later, as some aspirants themselves awakened and developed one sense after another, they have verified the truth of this information fact by fact, and though some still remains which they are *as yet* unable to verify, still they are naturally convinced of the truth of that which they have been told, for an error has never been found in the statement of a Master.

DEFINITION OF THEOSOPHY

We are now in a position to profit by a terse definition of Theosophy. The word itself is luminous and beautiful, signifying, as it does from its derivation, "wisdom concerning God." Apparently it was first used by Ammonius Saccas of Alexandria in the third century A.D., to designate an eclectic system of philosophy and oriental mysticism, which later developed into Neoplatonism. "Theosophy" has been variously defined but none of the definitions is ideal, though they all agree that Theosophy affirms the possibility of direct knowledge of "things divine and eternal."

Modern Theosophy may be defined as a synthesis of the essential truths of religion, science and philosophy. In presentation, it blends an adequate explanation of the problems and phenomena of life and the universe with a practical system of ethics and conduct arising naturally from such an explanation. Its statements, we have seen, are based upon a critical and comparative study of earlier theosophical, philosophical and religious systems, upon the discoveries of physical science, upon data obtained by trained superphysical perception, upon illumination resulting from awakened spiritual intuition, the whole of this mass of information being organized, bound together and supplemented by further information supplied by the Masters.

NATURE OF THEOSOPHY

It is evident, therefore, from a consideration of its sources, that *modern* Theosophy is not a revelation, in the accepted meaning of that word, and that, while its fundamental truths are rock-like because they are based upon reality, nevertheless the statements of its investigators as to details are not infallible. It is a growing system of thought, the result of careful study and research. Its ideal is to present things as they are and to eliminate speculation and theory. Mistakes may be made and have been made by its investigators, but they are corrected as soon as noticed. Such mistakes, as in scientific research, are due to incomplete observation and incorrect inference from what has been seen.

It should be remembered that, because of constant practice and effort, the powers of investigators are unfolding all the time, and that each year their capacity to observe is greater and more reliable. Naturally, therefore, the published investigations should and do show ever-increasing detail and precision as the years advance, and if one wishes to gain an adequate idea of the teachings of Theosophy, the later books should be read as well as the earlier ones. It is reassuring to note, however, that practically all the information obtained through modern theosophical investigation has stood the hard test of time, and that nearly all the changes made have been in the nature of amplifications. This speaks well for the accuracy of the theosophical researchers.

If Theosophy is what its friends claim it to be, then it is nothing less than the bedrock upon which all phases of the world's thought and activity are founded. Now such a body of knowledge is possible, theoretically, if the universe is a unity and not a chaos. Whether modern Theosophy is an approximation to that knowledge remains for time to prove.

2

THE OTHER WORLDS

On this matter of a larger, unseen world around us, I speak not at second hand, but partly of my own direct observation and knowledge. What there is peculiar in the centres of my brain I do not know; but a never-vanishing fact of my consciousness is that there is on all sides of me, through, within and without everything, an invisible world, which is most difficult to describe. . . . That world is luminous, and seems as if every point of its space was a point of self-created light of a kind different from the light of the physical world; . . . this invisible world has a greater reality than the physical world.

C. Jinarajadasa,
First Principles of Theosophy

2

THE OTHER WORLDS

NEW EXPLORATION

Though great rivers are still being discovered, the unexplored regions of the earth are shrinking year by year. This would be a matter only of congratulation were it not that our "natural-born travelers" will suffer the pangs of unsatisfied desire. How may that fever of discovery inherent in the race be cooled except by offering new realms for exploration? And where may those realms be found now that the visible earth has been raked, scraped, dissected, weighed and analyzed? Obviously we must turn our attention towards those other worlds to which seers have pointed for so many centuries without awakening much interest, it would seem, until now.

Advanced thinkers have already come to the conclusion that we are living not only on the surface of a

physical globe, but also in the midst of a normally unseen world. While many are beginning to suspect that
this subtle world may be studied scientifically, a few
are causing much shrugging of the shoulders by affirming that it has *already* been carefully investigated and
described, its inhabitants classified and its phenomena
tabulated. This statement is a strong one, we must admit, but it is made by those who have done the work
and denied by those who have not even taken the trouble to read the reports of the investigations. Now these
reports are exceedingly interesting and, while undoubtedly many details are lacking—for the study of a
new world is a Herculean task—nevertheless what has
been discovered instructs as well as fascinates.

ILLOGICAL ATTITUDES

Unfortunately, our understanding of this invisible
realm is oftentimes obscured because, strangely enough,
we usually adopt one of two attitudes, both of which
are illogical. Either we regard the whole matter as a
jumble of freakish fancies and the result of unwholesome speculation, or we swing to the other extreme
and veil everything related to this unseen realm in
unjustified mystery and reverence and speak of its
phenomena with bated breath. Mystery is the shadow
cast on nature by ignorance.

There seems to be an ingrained skepticism in most
people concerning anything nonphysical, frequently so
pronounced that it distorts their opinions and prevents
an unbiased judgment. This is certainly true when it
comes to consideration of the evidence for the existence of superphysical worlds. Many persons dogmati-
cally declare, without any investigation whatsoever,
that such worlds do not exist, not realizing that opin-

ions based on prejudices are valueless and that, as they are unacquainted with the numerous discoveries which have been made, their statements carry no weight whatever. It is significant that all those who have studied *carefully* the available evidence affirm their conviction that a nonphysical realm does exist.

LOCATION OF WORLDS

Theosophical investigation of this unseen realm has shown that it is composed of several interpenetrating regions or worlds, of which only two, however, are of practical importance in this preliminary study. These two subtle worlds are contained one within the other, the solid physical earth being embedded in the very heart of the two. We may think of them as two vast spheres surrounding the earth, not unlike a giant atmosphere, yet at the same time everywhere permeating the physical matter of the earth with the same ease that water vapor spreads through the air. One sphere is larger than the other and therefore extends much farther out into space, but both of them surround us all the time, although we are normally unconscious of their existence. As the earth swings through space following its pathway around the sun, these spheres move with it just as does the physical atmosphere.

Thus, strange as it may seem, we are living in several worlds at once, and we shall find, if we continue our studies, that human evolution is intimately connected with all of them. These subtle worlds are as objective and "real" to those conscious of them as the earth is "real" to us, and we should not think of them as shadowy unrealities because unknown to the physical senses. The matter of which they are formed is not physical in its characteristics. The matter in the two most accessible to us for want of better descriptive terms, has been called "emotional" and "mental" matter; the significance of these names will be seen later.

DISSECTION OF ATOM

The trend of recent scientific discoveries has been toward the infinitesimal—the dissection of the atom. Formerly it was believed that atoms were the ultimate units or bricks out of which all physical forms are built. Now it is known that the atoms themselves are complex structures, formed of differently grouped "bundles" of particles. Electrons are considered by many scientists to be not "things in themselves," but merely centers of force in the invisible electromagnetic field which surrounds and penetrates all things. Theosophical investigators, through direct observation made possible by certain awakened senses, have determined that every physical object, including the human body, is bathed and duplicated in "etheric" matter, through which flows continually electrical, magnetic and other forces closely associated with physical life. It was noticed that there were four densities or grades of this ether, which, with the familiar solids, liquids and gases, form seven densities of physical matter; for the ether itself is said to be physical, though invisible to the normal human eye.

This brings us to the important fact that there is no gulf between the physical and the next interpenetrating world. The matter of the denser world is formed indirectly out of the matter of the subtler. During the experiments of theosophical investigators, in which they studied the structure of matter, it was found that by a strong effort of the *will*—which set certain forces in action—it was possible to break up the particles of the

finest physical ether. When this was done the characteristics of the *resultant* particles entirely changed;
they were no longer physical in their nature. They
proved to be the molecules of the densest matter of the
interpenetrating subtle world.

ASTRAL WORLD

The molecules of the emotional or astral world obey
laws different from those governing physical matter.
They do not expand with heat nor contract with cold as
physical molecules do. They follow a law of gravity of
their own. The vibrations which move through them
permit an increased power of vision out of all proportion to physical sight. The matter itself is extremely
mobile, responding particularly in a most marvelous
way to the play of emotions—hence the name "emotional matter." Its response to emotion, desire and passion is greater than that of air to sound, for it carries
the vibrations a long distance from the person generating them and ripples into quivering masses of color
varying in hue according to the type of emotion. Another striking characteristic of this matter is that it is
readily molded by emotion into various forms which,
though evanescent, usually persist for several hours or
days, vibrating all the time at the same rate as the original oscillation which brought them into existence.

The densest matter of the emotional world duplicates
every physical object, so that it is possible while moving in its lower levels to observe what is taking place
physically. It is not that the physical objects themselves
are visible when one is observantly active in the emotional body, but the counterparts of those objects in
subtle matter are readily seen. In fact, those who are
not very observant or, for one reason or another, are

not aware that they are moving about in the astral world frequently do not detect any difference between objects formed of physical matter and the subtle duplicates of those objects. Farther out in those regions of the emotional world which are some distance from the surface of the earth, varied scenes of great beauty and interest are found—the products of the creative imagination of the people living there.

The emotional world is thickly populated with all types of living things, human and nonhuman, not on its surface as is the case with the earth, but within it as fish live in the sea and birds in the air. Limbs are not necessary for walking nor wings for flying, for *desire* and *will* are the motive powers which move us from place to place in this unseen world. Nevertheless we preserve the same appearance there as here, probably from habit, but also possibly from some deeper law of form which controls all creation.

The nonhuman creatures follow a line of evolution which has little to do directly with the human. They range in intelligence from the level of our lowest animals to lofty types far wiser than us—the angelic presences of religious tradition. They do not have physical bodies resembling ours, but appear in subtle bodies made of radiant emotional matter.

Animals who have lost their physical bodies by death are also there. They spend a brief though happy period in the emotional world before being born again of animals of the same species.

In this world are found millions of human beings, including not only the entire population that is living on earth at any one time—for, remember, we possess emotional bodies in addition to the physical—but also practically all those who have lost their physical bodies by death during the last thirty years. Those who have been "dead" longer than this have usually passed into the still more subtle world known as the mental or heaven world.

Lastly, contrasted with the millions of souls receiving their education on this planet a very small number of the Masters are found in the Astral world. They are the great Teachers mentioned so frequently in theosophical literature, and it is they who have charge of human evolution.

MENTAL WORLD

The mental or heaven world referred to is a much larger sphere, enveloping the physical earth and the emotional world, and yet at the same time interpenetrating the two. It may be reached therefore, not by moving in space, for it is all around us, but by learning to focus our consciousness in the "mental body" which is formed of its matter—a very difficult feat.

To realize again the close relationship between the different worlds, it should be noted that the exceedingly delicate matter of the mental world, which may truly be called "mind stuff," may be obtained by breaking up the finest matter of the emotional world. The mental world stands in the same relation to the emotional world as the latter does to the physical. Mental matter displays a set of characteristics all its own. It is marked chiefly by its instant response to the force of thought, breaking into cascades of restless, changing colors with every mental impulse. The matter is most luminous and beautiful as a result of its ceaseless vibrations. To quote the words of one investigator:

> These vibrations give rise to the most exquisite and constantly changing colors, waves of varying shades like the rainbow hues in mother-of-pearl, etherealized and

brightened to an indescribable extent, sweeping over and through every form, so that each presents a harmony of rippling, living, luminous, delicate colors, including many not known to earth. Words can give no idea of the exquisite beauty and radiance shown in combinations of this subtle matter, instinct with life and motion.*

In accordance with some process that is evidently intimately connected with the structural formation of the solar system, the matter of the mental world, in common with that of the emotional and of the physical world, is distinguished by seven grades or densities. In the mental world, however, there is an important division of these different grades of matter into two groups, the four denser grades forming collectively what is called the lower mental world, the three subtler, the higher mental world.

This is not an arbitrary division; it is based on certain differences in the matter itself. That of the lower mental world responds to what we call concrete thoughts and gives rise to mental images, pictures and forms; that of the higher mental world responds to our abstract thoughts by sending out waves of force in all directions.

There are almost countless intelligences dwelling in the heaven world. It is the realm of those lofty beings spoken of in sacred scriptures as angels or devas. It is also the true home of the Masters and their pupils, and it is here that they do most of their beneficent work of helping humanity in its age-long pilgrimage towards perfection.

The souls of all human beings are here—a vast host, some of them in physical incarnation, others resting and growing spiritually between one physical incarna-

*Annie Besant, The Ancient Wisdom, p. 146.

tion and the next. Since the heaven world is all around us, a soul never leaves that realm of bliss when taking an incarnation on earth; to form bodies, it merely gathers round itself the matter of the lower worlds with which it wishes to come into contact, and then trains those young bodies to respond to its more mature powers. As souls, we obtain only the *physical* body through the help of parents; the *mental* and *emotional* bodies we make for ourselves. Thus every moment of every day we, as souls, dwell in the heaven world; we are as much spirits now as we ever shall be, though it is true that much of our soul consciousness is cut off by the limitations of the brain.

3

THE AURA AND THE SOUL

*The larger, ovoid aura is an elaborate struc-
ture of lines of force which indicate both the
actual processes of thought and feeling from
moment to moment and the potentialities,
developed and undeveloped, of the spiritual
and psychic aspects of the individual. It is,
in short, a mirror in which the whole man
is reflected at every stage of his personal
development.*

*Laurence J. Bendit and
Phoebe P. Bendit
The Etheric Body of Man*

3

THE AURA AND THE SOUL

THE COLORED OVOID

The existence of an aura, or colored mist of rarefied matter surrounding the human body, has long been known. It was frequently depicted in paintings at the time of the Renaissance, not merely as a halo around the head, but as an ovoid in the midst of which the human form is standing. We have personally collected over sixty photographs of famous paintings now in Italian art galleries, in which the aura is shown.

The aura is clearly visible to the trained investigator and is frequently seen in part by many as a glow of light above the heads of others. All human beings, and to a certain extent animals, plants and even minerals, are surrounded and interpenetrated by a cloud of delicate matter drawn from the etheric part of the physical world and from the emotional and mental worlds. This matter is so sensitive that it responds instantly to thoughts and feelings, and as it does so its vibrations give rise to various colors.

In a developed human being this cloud of matter has become so specialized that it is to a large extent separated from the rest of the matter of the unseen world, in the same way that our physical bodies are distinct objects. Further, it is so molded and organized by the constant play of thoughts and feelings that it has been fashioned into subtle bodies by means of which a person comes into contact and communication with the invisible worlds.

ANALYSIS OF AURA

Analysis has shown that the aura is composed of four distinct layers:

(1) A striated etheric mist, bluish-grey in color, which extends outwards several inches on all sides from the surface of the skin. This is made up largely of etheric *emanations* from the etheric double of the physical body.

(2) An oval-shaped form, which is the seat of all our emotions, passions, feelings and sensations. This is the emotional body formed of the matter of the emotional world.

(3) A similarly shaped form, in which all our concrete, everyday thoughts and mental pictures are generated. This is the mental body formed of the matter of the lower mental world.

(4) An ovoid form, which is the seat of all our abstract and philosophical thoughts and spiritual aspirations. This is the causal body or soul body, formed of the matter of the higher mental world.

It is important to remember that these various bod-

ies, including the physical, are not separated like
pearls upon a string, but that they occupy the same
space, the subtler interpenetrating the denser ones,
the whole forming one compact working unit we call a
human being.

ETHERIC DOUBLE

The etheric double, which should not be confused
with the etheric emanations from it, is an exact counterpart of the physical body. It is faintly luminous and
bluish-grey in color and extends out beyond the surface
of the body about one-fourth of an inch and is sometimes visible to ordinary sight. It permeates the whole
physical body, and its function is to conduct different
currents of electricity, magnetism and vitality, which
circulate everywhere throughout the tissues.

The old idea, common a generation or so ago, that
there was a "vital force" is really nearer the truth than
many modern theories, for when one has developed
the power to see etherically, streams of rosy-colored
particles may be observed flowing down and around
each nerve from the brain, until, when they reach the
skin, they are forced out into the surrounding air. This
outrush of vitality particles from the nerve terminals in
the skin gives a striated appearance to the etheric atmosphere surrounding the body. Because the straight
or drooped arrangement of the striations indicates
whether a person is well or ill, it has frequently been
called the "health aura."

The rosy-colored particles are charged with a force
known as "vitality," which is distinct from electricity,
and is derived from the sun, for on bright days the air
is filled with colorless molecules charged with this

force, as if with myriads of dancing sparks of light. To be of use to the physical body, however, these colorless molecules must first be drawn into the etheric double in the neighborhood of the spleen and specialized into rosy-colored particles, which are then sent on their journey along the nerves and through the tissues of the body.

EMOTIONAL BODY

The emotional body is larger than its physical companion and on an average extends some eighteen inches around the latter on all sides. The emotional body of a person low on the ladder of evolution is a vaguely outlined, indefinite cloud of matter, glowing dully with muddy colors, but that of an advanced person is a sharply defined ovoid, marked by definite areas and bands, each one of which indicates a *habitual* trend of passion, feeling or emotion.

Despite the oval shape of the emotional body, it is interesting to know that in the emotional world we appear almost exactly as we do physically and are therefore easily recognizable. This is due to the fact that about ninety percent of the densest matter of the emotional body is condensed within the limits of the physical form, apparently being held there by some force of attraction, so that the oval form is only faintly indicated, while the denser counterpart of the physical body within is most prominent and clearly visible in every detail.

Whenever a strong emotion or feeling sweeps over a person, the emotional body is stirred to intense activity, and from its vibrating matter those colors flash out which are always associated with that emotion or feeling. Thus anger appears as scarlet, selfishness as a hard brown, fear as a livid grey, sympathy as a bright apple green, love as a tint of rose, devotion as blue, and so on. The study of these colors and their correspondences to the changes of consciousness is one of the most interesting of the many aspects of Theosophy.

MENTAL BODY

The mental body is usually of the same size as the emotional, both of them growing in size as we advance along the path of evolution. With definite progress in the power to think, the mental body becomes more highly organized and therefore more definite in outline. It is exceedingly luminous and radiant with clear, beautiful colors, especially in an advanced type of human being, each color area indicating a *habitual* thought attitude.

The vibrations which accompany intellectual activity emit a yellow light, which varies in hue from a strong orange-yellow in a commonplace, selfish type of mind to the beautiful primrose yellow of the philosophical mind of an advanced person. All our mental activity which can be expressed in images and pictures arises here, for the mental body is the conscious instrument used in generating concrete thoughts.

THE SOUL OR EGO

Lastly we come to the true man, the soul, of whom it is said in the *Bhagavad Gita*:

He is not born, nor doth he die, nor having been ceaseth he any more to be. Unborn, perpetual, eternal and ancient, he is not slain when the body is slaughtered.

This passage refers to the individuality, the soul, who survives all bodily changes, stores up all experiences and remembers all events. It is our higher Self, the source of that sense of "I" which is always in the background of all our thinking.

The form of the causal body is ovoid—in fact it is the mold upon which the mental and emotional bodies are fashioned—and while in one who is unevolved it resembles an empty bubble because undeveloped, in the advanced person it is marvelously beautiful, flashing with radiant colors and glowing with a living light, all its own. Words are powerless to describe this; it must be seen to be known.

The growth of the soul is almost inconceivably slow during the early stages of human evolution, because the only experiences upon which the soul can thrive are fine emotions, inspiring thoughts and unselfish aspirations. Naturally these are almost unknown while humans are still learning the crude lessons of physical existence, but they come later when we commence to turn our attention to higher things. This is the enormous advantage of living a pure and noble life, dedicated to unselfish service—it gives to the soul, the real person that which stimulates growth in a most wonderful manner and hastens one's journey to the splendid goal of human evolution.

EFFECTS OF THOUGHT AND EMOTION

Whenever we think or feel, our invisible bodies vibrate strongly, and as they do so they produce two effects in the atmosphere of the subtle worlds:

(1) They set up waves which radiate out from us in all directions, not unlike circular water waves on the surface of a pond after the fall of a pebble. But it should

be remembered that thought waves move out as rapidly expanding spheres of which we form the center, not merely as increasing circles. The distance to which these waves penetrate is proportionate to the intensity of the thought or emotion which created them; a strong thought sends out a powerful wave, a weak thought a feeble wave which soon flickers out.

These thought- and emotion-waves affect the thoughts and feelings of everyone they touch more or less and tend to stir up similar, but not exact, reproductions of the impulse which started them on their journey. Thus a feeling of depression over some personal failure will tend to reproduce similar feelings of depression in the emotional bodies of many people within a certain radius, but each person so affected will associate the depression with some trouble which he or she has experienced and not with the trouble of the sender. In the same way a strong thought of joy will cause many in the immediate neighborhood to feel joyous, though they know not why, usually connecting the emotion that surges into their thoughts with some happy event which happened not long before.

(2) A strong emotion or thought actually builds a little form in the subtle matter of the unseen worlds and projects it with the rapidity of a rifle bullet to the object or person with whom the thought was connected. This thought-form may persist for many hours or even days, depending upon the intensity of the original impulse, and its one function is to impress upon the subtle bodies of the distant person the exact thought or emotion which brought it into existence. This once accomplished and its force discharged, it melts away again into the sea of surrounding matter as a cloud melts into the blue sky. But for a time it was almost a living thing, charged with thought energy.

If the thought or emotion is personal and not connected with another, the thought-form generated lingers around its creator, and during some moment when the consciousness of the latter is passive, discharges its energy upon him or her. Thus many of the thoughts which tempt us are those we ourselves generated a few hours or days before.

These facts indicate how we may be of much service to others by the assistance and encouragement we can give them with our thoughts. Furthermore, it warns us to be on our guard as to the kind of thoughts we permit in our minds and to the quality of emotions we allow ourselves to feel. For our thoughts and feelings create a very real personal atmosphere through the influence of which we help or hinder those with whom we come in contact.

SLEEP

Whenever we go to sleep, we withdraw from our physical bodies and move about in the unseen world, using our emotional bodies. People are not equally conscious, however, while their physical bodies are asleep. The extent to which we are aware that we are in an unseen world depends primarily upon the stage of growth we have reached as souls and secondarily upon our physical-brain knowledge of the existence of that world.

The consciousness of dense and ignorant persons is so undeveloped, that, during the hours of sleep when they are no longer experiencing the stir and rush of physical life, they are practically unconscious as they float in their cloudy emotional bodies just above their slumbering physical bodies. People of a little more developed type, are actively conscious in their emotional bodies while their physical bodies sleep but they know nothing of the unseen world, as they are completely absorbed in thinking over their own petty plans and dreaming about the objects of their desires. At a still further state of development, glimpses of the outside emotional world are caught now and then, and such a person may move some distance away from the slumbering body in search of these half-glimpsed adventures and scenes.

Thoughtful, cultured people, however, especially those who have had some training as occultists, are very active in the emotional world, meeting many people, visiting distant places and going through interesting experiences. If willing, they may be a power there for good, teaching, helping and protecting those who know much less than they. This is the beneficent work of those known as the "invisible helpers."

Those whom we mistakenly call "dead" are quite active in the emotional world for several years after the death of their physical bodies, and it is possible for us to meet and talk with them at night. Death is a separation only in our imaginations, for every night of our lives we are with those who have passed on and whom we love.

DREAMS AND MEMORIES

Sometimes when we awake in the morning we remember with singular vividness some scene, experience or conversation. Such a dream is usually a memory of something which has actually happened to us while we were out of our physical bodies. We should remember, however, that we may be very active in the emotional world at night and yet when we awake retain not a single memory of what we have done. This is entirely due to the insensitiveness of the brain.

The usual dreams, which are grotesque, fantastic and illogical, arise spontaneously in the brain itself while we are away from it. They are usually fragments of pictures or experiences automatically reproduced by the brain cells during the absence of any guiding intelligence, and their very absurdity shows that the brain is merely an instrument of consciousness, not an originator of thought.

It is helpful if we clearly understand that our waking consciousness—that is, the totality of the thoughts and feelings of which we are aware while awake—is only a small portion of our whole consciousness. In fact, our waking consciousness is made up of only those *overtones* arising in the grey matter of the brain by sympathetic response to the more powerful vibrations of the emotional and mental bodies, the seats respectively of our emotional natures and minds. In the great majority of cases, because of general lack of development, lack of training and care in diet, the nervous tissue is not very responsive, and as a result of the very limitations of the brain as a transmitting instrument, we are aware in our waking consciousness of only a small portion of all our emotions and thoughts.

4

WHAT HAPPENS AFTER DEATH

The answer to that is found partially in the great religions of the world, but they are very various in their statements, as might be expected. Sometimes even within their own limits they contradict each other, but on one point they are entirely at one, and that is that there is a life on the other side of death. There is one very fine phrase that you may read in Hebrew Scripture, put among the Apocrypha (I do not know why), in which a key to the riddle is offered to you, and that phrase is: "God created man to be immortal, and made him in the image of His own eternity."

Annie Besant, The Theosophist,
Vol. 55, No 8, May, 1934

4

WHAT HAPPENS AFTER DEATH

THE ILLUSION OF DEATH

Death is an episode, not a tragedy; it is liberation from the physical body and not the annihilation of the consciousness. Though death may take from us our outworn or outgrown bodies, it grants us the wider freedom of the unseen worlds, and to those who know, death has no terrors—not one. Instead of being a dark-robed king of terrors, death is a bright Presence bearing the blessed key which unlocks the prison house of the flesh; and it would be well for us to learn the truth about what happens after death and then to cast aside forever all grief and mourning—twin offsprings of ignorance.

There is a foolish aphorism current among us that all are equal in the grave—king and beggar, sage and fool. This is perhaps true of their physical bodies, but it is a mistake so far as they themselves are concerned. We are unchanged by death; our powers of consciousness may indeed become somewhat greater and the extent of our vision and perception larger, but we are the same people after death as before—mentally, morally and spiritually. Death cannot transform us into something different just because it strikes away the physical instrument, the body, we have used on earth. It cannot suddenly convert us into prayerful saints or all-wise spirits; such changes can come about only during the long course of evolution. After death we cling to the same follies, believe the same half-truths, display the same prejudices and associate with the same sorts of people that we did while in physical incarnation.

True, we know a little more because we are surrounded by the phenomena of a larger world, and we are at least convinced that death does not end all because we ourselves have survived it. But on the other hand, few people are careful observers, and so the knowledge we obtain after death is usually general and not detailed, and further, it is often distorted by our beliefs and prejudices.

THE ACT OF DYING

The act of dying and of going to sleep are similar except in a few particulars. In both cases we withdraw from the physical body. When we go to sleep the etheric matter in the physical body remains unchanged, and therefore while we are absent the currents of vitality play through the body and keep it alive. But when we die the etheric double goes out with us, the currents of vitality, which flow in ether, cease, and the physical body becomes cold and motionless, even though all its organs may be unimpaired. As

soon as the etheric matter withdraws, the slow disinte-
gration of the cells commences and decay sets in.

As we withdraw from the physical body at the time of
death, we are surrounded by the etheric matter which
came out with us. This envelops us like a fog and prevents us from obtaining even a glimpse of the astral
world, which surrounds us with its multifarious activities and interests. As a result, most of us during this
period, which lasts several hours, are entirely unconscious of our condition and environment.

AFTER-DEATH EXPERIENCE

After a time this etheric matter slowly slips away and
we become more and more aware of the emotional
world of which we are now a conscious inhabitant.
Since every physical object is duplicated in emotional
matter, we are apt at first, particularly if we are not
very observant, to notice very little difference between
this new world and the physical earth. Indeed, it is difficult at times to convince some people that they are
really "dead," for they are frequently possessed of such
fantastic ideas as to what *ought* to happen but which
does not happen after death that it takes several days
to persuade them that they have really lost their physical bodies.

However, after a few attempts to eat and walk and
talk as they were accustomed to do on earth, these obstinate people begin to realize that *something is wrong*.
They eat the food of which they think and therefore
immediately see before them, but for some reason it
has no taste and does not give them any satisfaction. It
is only gradually that they realize they are no longer in
their physical bodies. They have still to learn that the
astral body does not require food. They walk about

among their old haunts and homes but find themselves unable to move certain objects as before. They have still to find out that a person living in the unseen world cannot move *physical* objects merely by trying to lift their astral counterparts.

The newly deceased talk to others they meet and are very much puzzled at first to notice that while they can converse with some people at any hour, other persons will only pay attention to them about eight hours out of twenty-four. During the rest of the time these peculiar men and women—for as such they are considered by the obstinate "dead" people whose experiences we are studying—do not respond to anything which is said. Our friends in the emotional world have still to discover that, while they can mingle and speak at any time with other people who are also "dead," they cannot gain the attention of those in physical incarnation during the hours when the latter are awake, that is, when the consciousness is focused in the physical brain. Only when the physical bodies of people in incarnation go to sleep are they released from the limitations of the brain and therefore responsive to astral surroundings.

As we gain more experience in this life we are leading after death, we learn many other important lessons and facts. For some time we are apt to believe it necessary to walk about as we did on earth, to regard a door as something to be opened before we can pass through and to think of walls as being impassable barriers. After a time we find that we can pass through any of these seemingly solid things without the least difficulty, and that, when we desire to go to a distant place, there is not the slightest necessity for *walking* there. All we need do is to will strongly to go to that place; there is a sense of motion, and we find ourselves there.

One of the most common dreams is that of flying—either of moving through the air or skimming along the ground, taking only a running step now and then. From questions put to audiences in many cities, it has been found that about twenty-five to forty percent of intelligent people have dreams of this description. Such dreams of flying are merely indications that we are learning how to move about in the way which is normal in the emotional world.*

We also realize after death that every uncontrolled passion and appetite of the ignoble sort, which we allowed to fasten upon us during our life on earth, is something for which we must *now* pay the price. The cravings which we were accustomed to gratifying without question can no longer be satisfied because our physical bodies are gone. All the passions and desires are still as strong as before, and there is nothing to do now but to live them down and let them die out for want of gratification. We bitterly regret that we did not know this before death because the bite of an unsatisfied desire is now far stronger than it was when we were living in the physical body, for this is the world of feeling. Any hell that is to be found after death is one which we make for ourselves by what we do and feel and think while on earth; we are not punished by any external power, we punish ourselves.

THE HARM OF GRIEF

We also see how utterly wrong it is to give way to uncontrolled grief for those who are "dead," for now we, who have lost our physical bodies by death, are

---

See C. W. Leadbeater, *The Chakras* (Wheaton: Theosophical Publishing House, 1974), p. 78.

continually surrounded by the almost unbearable thoughts of grief and passionate longing created by our loving but misguided friends who are mourning our death. Strangely enough, though these same friends are with us and talk with us while their physical bodies are asleep, just as soon as they awake in the morning they revert to the old delusion that they have lost us and think thoughts of bitter sorrow all day long. We stand beside them and cry out that we are there, but they do not hear us or even feel our presence because their nervous systems are so insensitive and their attention is so fully directed to worldly affairs. They make us, the dead, very unhappy and miserable by their illogical and foolish attitude, and we can really only gain relief from this intolerable condition when they begin to *forget* us and think of other things. Be under no delusion that grief or mourning gratify the "dead"; it only makes them miserable. Why cannot people realize that all such sorrowing is *wrong*, that uncontrolled grief makes life a hell for us who are living in the emotional world, and that there is really no separation since those who love us are with us every night while their physical bodies are asleep and resting. God did not design this world to be a torture chamber. The source of all sorrow is ignorance, if we only knew it.

PROGRESS AFTER DEATH

As the years roll on—counting time as is done on earth—we find that more radiant and beautiful regions of this emotional world unfold before our gaze, and we are startled to discover that we have been surrounded by these glorious regions all the time but did not know it, because of a peculiarity of the emotional body. It seems that it can only respond to the vibrations of the emotional world outside it according to the degree of sensitiveness of the matter on its *surface*. If this surface layer is coarse, we sense only slow vibrations such as are characteristic of the lower levels of the emotional world; if fine, then the swifter vibrations of the higher levels will bring their messages to our consciousness.

We are told that a curious rearrangement of the matter of the emotional body takes place immediately after our death. By an instinctive effort of the emotional body, the matter composing it is thrown into concentric layers, the coarsest on the outside, the finest within, various other grades lying between the two. This arrangement is unnecessary and we can stop it if we know that it is taking place. But if we do not know, the emotional body instinctively sorts out its matter in this way and thereby prolongs its existence.

This rearrangement causes us to be conscious only on that level of the emotional world corresponding in density to the matter on the surface of the emotional body. Hence, because our life on earth may not have been all that it should, we do not have a very high opinion, at first, of this emotional world because we are limited to a rather low level for a while. In fact, some of us may have a rather uncomfortable time during the first few months because we have built a considerable amount of coarse matter into our emotional bodies by unwholesome habits and impure diets. When this finally wears away, we then become conscious of much more pleasant regions.

The opening up of new vistas of beauty and enjoyment is continually taking place with every person as the coarser particles are gradually eliminated from the emotional body. And after we have lived in this world several years, our interest in worldly affairs wanes because there are so many more interesting things to attend to here. While we still love the people who are yet in physical incarnation, nevertheless we realize sensibly that they must live their lives as we lived ours, and that we really only hinder them by trying to interfere. Further, as we become conscious of the more beautiful levels of the emotional world, the duplicates of physical objects gradually become less prominent, and so little by little we lose touch with earth life and turn our thoughts to higher and more important things. We become more introspective and begin to learn the value of our own thoughts.

LIFE IN HEAVEN

Eventually there comes a time when we slowly awaken to a new glory of life and color which is beyond all words to describe. So intense is our bliss that it does not even interest us to know that we have now cast off the useless emotional body—which speedily disintegrates—and are living in our radiant mental body in the heaven world. In the words of one who has learned to lift the consciousness, even while functioning in the brain, to this supernal world, a person who withdraws into the heaven-world "awakens to a sense of joy unspeakable, of bliss immeasurable, of peace that passeth understanding. Softest melodies are breathing around him, tenderest hues greet his opening eyes, the very air seems music and color, his whole being is suffused with light and harmony. Then through the golden haze dawn sweetly the faces loved on earth, etherealized into beauty which expresses their noblest, loveliest emotions, unmarred by the troubles and passions of the lower worlds. Who may tell the bliss of that awakening, the glory of that first dawning of the heaven-world?"

Many centuries may be spent in this world of happiness engaged in assimilating the experiences gained on earth and transmuting their essence into wisdom and faculty. This world is our true home, and here we enjoy the fruits gathered during our visit to earth. The time spent here is a period of inner growth, and the food we consume is the harvest of good thoughts, emotions and aspirations, which we sowed during the earth life. The heaven life is one of intense, unalloyed happiness, without even the shadow of a sorrow.

After a period in the lower heaven-world, the length of which is determined by the stage of evolution we have reached as souls and the amount of experience we gained during our life on earth, the time comes when we have thought over every fragment of experience, carried out every spiritual aspiration, lived through every joy, accomplished everything possible in this world, of which we can conceive. At that moment the now useless mental body drops away, and our consciousness suddenly expands to that of the mature soul, our true inner Self. Then we realize our divine nature; then we remember the long path we have trodden to gain our present stage of evolution; then we recall the past lives we have lived on earth; for the causal body is the storehouse of all memories and it never forgets, though the brain and lower mind may be ignorant of the past.

RETURN TO BIRTH

For varying lengths of time we live in this condition of pure soul consciousness. The unevolved soul has but a flash of this lofty condition; an advanced philosopher may enjoy this state for years and even centuries. But with all, the time inevitably comes when there is awakened a thirst for more experience, for activity, for increased knowledge of details *such as may only be gained on earth,* and with that dawning desire, the soul turns its consciousness once more towards the lower worlds. First it draws round itself a cloud of matter of the lower mental world, out of which, during the childhood of its future physical body, it fashions a mind body; then it gathers to itself a cloud of matter of the emotional world, which later is molded into an emotional body; lastly it becomes linked to an infant body provided by parents with whom the soul has formed ties in previous lives on earth. And thus it is that a new incarnation commences as the child is born, a child with its as yet unorganized emotional and mental bodies, through which, as the years advance, the mature soul behind is able to manifest its powers more and more.

5

GROWTH THROUGH REINCARNATION

The soul incarnates many times for the sake of experience, and each one will thereby become at last not merely a genius in some field of human thought or work, but a perfect man, ready for full conscious divinity.

Annie Besant and
C. W. Leadbeater,
Talks on the Path of Occultism

5

GROWTH THROUGH REINCARNATION

THE WORLD SCHOOL

One of the most illuminative and helpful of the teachings of Theosophy is that this world, with all its activities and interests, is in reality a great educational institution in which millions of souls and countless other creatures are receiving the instruction which they need for their growth. We learn that there are many more human beings connected with the earth than ever appear in incarnation at any one time, but that all are enabled to gain the experiences they need by making a short visit periodically to this world, thereby coming in contact with the lessons taught by civilization.

Thus each life spent here is merely a day in the greater soul life, and each time we return we resume our lessons about where we left off before, aided, of course, by what we have gained by home study—for heaven is the home of the soul. The young soul is commencing education in the kindergarten of life; the spiritually developed person is nearing the time of graduation from this world school; the rest of us are standing on some step between these two extremes. We have gleaned much experience from hundreds of lives in the past—that is why we are as advanced as we are; and in the future new lives will help us complete and round out our education.

This view of human life and of the growth of the soul is called "reincarnation" or "rebirth," and in a more or less pure form is the working philosophy of millions of human beings today, particularly in the Orient. As a philosophical conception it is hoary with age and has apparently held the attention, by its logic and inherent reasonableness, of many of the great leaders of thought during all periods of history.

SCHOOLBOY LOGIC

Yet many persons, when they first hear of reincarnation, reject the idea without any consideration and exclaim: "What a horrible belief! I am sure I don't want to come back again!" And for some reason such people, who are otherwise sensible enough, seem to think that their dislike of reincarnation proves it untrue and unnecessary.

But does dislike of teaching make it unnecessary? Does the rebellion of the small boy who is kept by his parents at school make his education any less essential? In later years does not this same small boy look back upon his rebellious feelings with a smile of amusement at his short-sightedness? And may we not as souls, look back upon this time when we are seeking to avoid the priceless lessons of life and smile at our own ignorance and lack of understanding of the purpose of existence?

Are we actually opposed to reincarnation *as such*? Let us suppose that this earth is a glorious paradise in which sorrow, suffering and trouble are unknown. When death claimed us, would we not be overcome with despair at leaving this land of bliss? If someone said that rebirth is a possibility, we would leap at the chance and offer premiums to get back to earth! If we are perfectly frank with ourselves, we must admit that we are not objecting to reincarnation merely as a process of being born again; what we wish to avoid are the many trials, difficulties and sorrows of physical existence. We want to escape experience, not rebirth!

Yet those very experiences which we seek to escape, those very sorrows and difficulties and trials, have taught us some of the grandest and deepest lessons of life and have forced us to awaken many a power of consciousness and will that otherwise would never have been stimulated to activity. The hardships of civilization have made us what we are, while ease and luxury only sap our courage and deaden our initiative. A person who has never suffered or failed or felt sorrow is a person without much sympathy, compassion, or real understanding of life.

Obviously, then, our emotional objections to reincarnation are hopelessly illogical and childish, and as thoughtful people we should not permit our dislike of the teaching process to carry away our reason and good sense.

LOGIC OF REINCARNATION

The idea of reincarnation is exceedingly logical, whether we admit it to be a fact in nature or not. It offers to the growing soul, not the paltry gains of a single life on earth, but unlimited experience in many stations of life and under all possible circumstances. Not a single event can happen to us that does not offer something of value for growth, even though the drop of wisdom which may be distilled from it is small.

By varying the conditions of birth and the occupation from life to life, lopsided development can be prevented and all-round knowledge of the world obtained. Thus if this life we are now leading is but one of a series, such experience, no matter how trivial, is valuable; but if this is the only life we live on earth, then we must frankly admit that much that we experience and learn here is practically useless in the future, for the knowledge gained would be of value only on earth and not in any heaven-world. If we return we can make good use of that knowledge, but if we do not then many of our efforts and lessons gained at great cost are just so much wasted time.

Furthermore, what is the value of physical existence to a soul who inhabits the body of an infant that lives but a few hours or the body of a child criminal born and reared in the slums? If we live but one life, there is no satisfactory explanation; but if this life is one of many arranged in an ascending series, then we see in the two conditions just mentioned the payment of a debt, in one case, and the first efforts of an ignorant untaught soul, in the other.

CURRENT MISCONCEPTIONS

One of the current misconceptions about reincarnation, which prevents a consideration of the idea by thoughtful people, is that it teaches the return of a human being to the body of an animal—that next life we may be born as a dog or a horse! This point of view is obviously so absurd that it seems foolish to mention it; yet people who ought to know better seriously advance it as an argument against reincarnation. It is as sensible to speak of transferring a college student to a kindergarten class in order to recommence his education as it is to think of a human soul being born again in the body of an animal. Nature is never so unreasonable as this!

Progress is forwards, not backwards, so as we advance we always come back in human bodies, each one a little better than the previous one. Sometimes, it is true, for some grievous fault, we may during one incarnation retrace our steps to a slight extent and take birth in a less advanced type of body and under less favorable conditions. But this retrograde movement is only apparent and not real, even as the backward movement of an eddy in the flowing water of a river does not change the forward course of the stream.

Another misconception is that we are reborn immediately. Careful investigation has shown, however, that this rarely happens and that the normal interval between one life and another varies from a few score years in the case of an undeveloped soul to twenty centuries or even more in the case of a far advanced type. The length of this interval depends primarily upon the amount of experience gained during the earth life, and this in turn depends upon three factors:

(1) The length of the physical life—the longer the life, the more experience.

(2) The quality of the life. Some lives are tranquil and placid, while others are adventurous and crowded with events. Naturally the latter supply more experience.

(3) The age of the soul. We did not commence our evolution at the same time and may therefore be sorted

out theoretically into classes, as with children in a school; hence we are not all of the same educational age. The older the soul, the less it engages in purely physical pursuits and the more it is interested in mental, moral and spiritual things. Naturally, activities of the latter type, inasmuch as they are expressions of our larger life in the subtler worlds, give us more to think over and assimilate during the interval between one life and the next.

THREE THEORIES

There are three possible theories to account for the soul before it commenced its life here at birth:

(1) It was newly created by God at birth—a point of view commonly held in Christian countries. This is the theory of special creation.

(2) It existed before birth in some spiritual state but has never lived before on earth. This is the theory of pre-existence.

(3) It has lived many times before on earth, and its capacities and abilities are the results of that past experience. This is the theory of reincarnation.

One of these three theories must be right, and it is our duty carefully to study the facts of life until we can determine which one is true. If we love truth, prejudice should not blind us, nor should the traditional beliefs, held without question by those around, deter us from forming our own independent opinions.

DIVINE JUSTICE

One of the hardest problems for a humane person to solve is the reconciliation of the heart-breaking injustice of many of the conditions of this world with a belief in the perfect justice and love of God. Some souls are born in slums and taught nothing but crime; others are reared in refined families and tenderly guarded by loving fathers and mothers. Why? Some are born into crippled and diseased bodies, others into bodies that are perfect. Why? Some are born as idiots, while others are gifted with brilliant intellectual powers. Again, why?

We may, of course, explain all of these conditions to our own satisfaction on the basis of physical heredity and the responsibility of parents, but does this make the situation any more just so far as the *souls* themselves are concerned? They are the ones who suffer, not the parents, and if we are to see God's justice in the world, we must understand why they suffer as they do.

Many people are unwilling to admit that God is unjust, and so, because they are unable to justify the actual facts spread out before their eyes, fall back on the statement that all these conditions are the workings of an *inscrutable* Providence whose ways we may not question. This, of course, is not an explanation of the conditions; it is an admission of ignorance. Nor is there any ground for the hope in the light of the first two theories, a conclusion expressed by many persons who claim that although there is undoubtedly much injustice and undeserved suffering in the world, death will surely square all and we shall receive our due recompense on the other side of the grave. Have we any justification for this hope? If God created a world so imperfectly conceived that rampant injustice is found everywhere, how do we know that the same state of affairs does not prevail after death?

JUSTICE AND REINCARNATION

But there is a line of reasoning which carries us out of this intolerable situation and illuminates all our human problems. We may reduce this reasoning to a very simple statement:

Life is unjust if we experience any undeserved suffering or unearned happiness.

Much comes to us which we have neither earned nor deserved in this life.

Therefore, if a just God exists, we must have lived on earth before and during that time started the causes which now are controlling circumstances.

We may expand this line of reasoning and approach the problem from a slightly different angle:

This life is a living hell if we are the innocent victims of a Power which is either so merciless, unjust or weak, that it is unable to control the world it has created.

Unless the extent to which our capacities and abilities and the opportunities which come to us are the direct results of our own efforts and therefore deserved, we are such victims.

But if we are not victims and these conditions were caused by ourselves, then we must have lived on earth before, or in some condition exactly resembling physical existence, in order to have sown the seeds we are now reaping as harvests.

If we refuse to be false to our intuition that God is absolutely just, the conclusion is inevitable that reincarnation is the true theory regarding the soul. Theosophy is unassailable when it affirms that there is no injustice anywhere in the universe, and that every event of life—when we can see the whole of it—is in reality part of the working of a perfect law of cause and effect which is flawless in its justice. We call an event unjust because we are looking only at the result and

have not the power to turn back the pages of history
and see the cause.

OTHER ARGUMENTS

But there are also other facts which indicate that reincarnation is a law of nature. Notice the enormous differences in mental and moral faculties between one
person and another. Education and environment cannot
account for all the difference. Someone who has grown
up in tribal life without being touched by the least ves-
tige of civilization can be taught modern ways and
moved into advantageous surroundings. While there
would be impressive progress, such a person's advancement would not be parallel to one who had been born
and grown up with the same advantages.

It is not a question of physical heredity alone. In the
case of twins, born under exactly the same prenatal in-
fluences, the most striking differences in ability and
character are frequently noticed after a few years. This
would not be the case if physical heredity were the
only factor at work.

If we understand that the souls themselves differ in
experience, that some are just commencing their school-
ing while others are near graduation, then these differences are easily and logically explained. Physical
heredity no doubt plays an important part so far as the
quality and appearance of our physical bodies are concerned, but we are born with our emotional and mental powers in the form of innate faculties. Whence
come the faculties of the "born" teacher, speaker, or
leader? Often the parents and even the ancestors do
not display them. How explain the occurrence of a Na-
poleon, a Shakespeare, a Wagner? The most careful
tracing of their ancestry leaves us more puzzled than

before, if physical heredity is the sole factor.

What is the source of genius? Can water rise higher than its source? If not, why should offspring be greater than their parents and ancestors? But if geniuses are old souls who have developed enormous capacity along a certain line—music, drama, painting, mathematics— then we need not strain to apply the theory of physical heredity in order to explain their appearance in the world. Reincarnation also shows why the sons and daughters of a genius are never equal to the parent. Geniuses can only transmit their physical peculiarities to their offspring, never their inspiring talents, which are the powers of the soul.

MEMORIES OF PAST LIVES

An objection frequently made to the idea of reincarnation is that if we have lived before we would have memories of the past. The argument which the objector has in mind runs something like this: We remember whatever we have experienced; we have no memories of past lives; therefore we have not lived before.

This reasoning is exceedingly faulty because it leaves out of account that physically we forget experience more than we remember it. How many of us can remember exactly what we did and said twelve years ago this day? Not one. How many of us can remember everything we did last week, or even yesterday? Major events, yes, but not details. Why? Because the memories have been lost forever? No, only because the physical brain cannot recall them. If we are thrown into a hypnotic trance state by a psychologist, we can easily be helped to recall everything we have done in the past, the extent to which we are able to recover these old memories depending upon the depth of the trance. *This is absolute proof that every one of us possesses millions of memories of which the physical brain has no recollection whatsoever.* Obviously the argument advanced against reincarnation is not sound, for there may exist a deep layer of our consciousness in which adhere the memories of other lives on earth—memories entirely unknown to the waking consciousness.

This at least is the statement of theosophical investigators, and their conclusions are borne out by numerous experiments in hypnotic regression in which memories of past lives have been found to agree with facts about the era in history of the supposed incarnation. Further, it should not be forgotten that some people do remember their past lives, at least in part, and in making this statement we do not have in mind those persons who imagine themselves to have been Anthony or Cleopatra or some other romantic character. Children frequently have glimpses of other lives and strive to tell us of them, but we laugh and call them fancies, and the child soon forgets, especially as it grows older and the brain tissue becomes less plastic to "far memory" as it has been called. Ian Stevenson, psychiatrist from the University of Virginia, has made careful studies and verified many cases of this type.

Reincarnation is not an endless process, any more than we go to school all our life. It ceases when we have learned all the major lessons this world can teach us and we have reached the stage of perfection. Then we are ready to assume the greater duties and commence the wider work for which our education in the world-school has fitted us. For just as we go forth into the world after our school days are over, so do we venture into a larger field after our many lives on earth are ended. The analogy is exact.

6

THE PROBLEM OF DESTINY

. . . the karma that you are making every day is modifying all the results of the karma of the past. It is a continuing creation, and not something lying in wait for us; it is not a sword hanging over us that may drop on us at any moment.

Annie Besant
The Theosophic Life

6

THE PROBLEM OF DESTINY

THE PURPOSE OF EXPERIENCE

We measure life by false standards, by pleasure and pain and not by growth. If life is pleasant, we bless destiny, if unpleasant we curse it, never considering in either case whether we grow through the experiences that come. Destiny is nature's plan of education; she is not trying to please us, to kill time, to furnish a continual round of pleasure; she is endeavoring to teach us. That is why we must work, endure hardships, struggle for what we get. Rugged lessons truly, but wonderfully effective in their results, for such teaching as we receive on earth produces strong men and brave women, not weaklings. Even though lives are spent in learning lessons, they are eventually mastered, for in this world-school there are no failures.

Destiny, however, offers many problems, and the greatest of them is to find the cause of the fate which brings us to our parents, determines our opportunities, gauges our faculties and molds our lives. To a certain extent this problem was considered in the last chapter, but we must go further. Over the centuries three answers have been proposed to explain human destiny. Let us consider these answers in turn.

DESTINY THE WILL OF GOD

The first answer is that our lives are molded at the dictates of some Being who is the ruler of the universe. At his command all things come or are withheld. We are like puppets moved by an unseen hand across a stage; we act, but the scenes, the actors, our very characters and the events which happen are all prescribed by him. If he wills it, we may be exalted in the eyes of our fellows; if it is his wish, we may be disgraced and shamed. No exertion can change our destiny; that rests with him. We have neither earned the happiness nor deserved the suffering which is our portion, for our destinies are decided on high.

This may be considered an exaggerated statement of a particular viewpoint, yet this is exactly what is *implied* in the resigned acceptance of one who murmurs as many of us have done after a blow has fallen, "Thy will be done." Yet how hard it is to think that all we see happening around us is due to God's will. We ask ourselves if it is true that he blinds children, breaks the hearts of strong men, permits people to be sent to prison, though innocent of crime, creates a world in which souls fresh from his hands may be born in crippled or idiotic bodies and babes may become diseased for the sins of their *parents*. If we dare not go to the extreme of saying that he does all this, then we are merely avoiding the inevitable outcome of a consistent application of this answer to destiny.

But if God deliberately causes such suffering or *even permits it to happen* to the souls concerned without justification, how can we reverence him? What purpose is there in it all? We do not know why we came here; we do not know where we are to go; and during our stay on earth we are unjustly treated. The future is uncertain, without promise, for if he allows destiny to crush our neighbor, may he not permit the same awful fate to visit us? We must submit to every caprice, for destiny cannot be controlled by us but only by him.

Is this a satisfactory answer to the problem? Emphatically it is not, and surely it is accepted blindly by so many only because they refuse even to think about its unreasonableness, believing that no other solution exists and fearing that if they trust themselves to the stormy sea of doubt, they may be lost.

DESTINY THE RESULT OF CHANCE

According to the second answer to the problem of destiny, life is merely the product of circumstances, the result of chance. There may or may not be a God, but if one does exist, he does not concern himself very closely with the world he has created, and may therefore be left out of account so far as destiny is concerned. We may be born in the hovel of peasants or in the home of refined parents, for there is no choice or law governing birth, and the soul must accept what it receives. Human bodies are born because their parents are swayed by passion. We have done nothing to deserve our birth conditions or environment; in fact, from the viewpoint of this answer to destiny, it is absurd to speak of the events of life which happen to us as expressing any purpose; they merely happen. Luck rules—chance is king.

Assuredly, we can never be certain of results. We may toil for years only to fail in the end, or we may win by a lucky move. All talk of rewards and punishments is idle. We are but gamblers spinning the wheel of fortune; if we pick the right color we succeed; if we make a mistake, we lose. All we can do is to strive to win and then anxiously await the next turn of the wheel, for there is no law, no certainty.

This is surely a tottering foundation upon which to build the structure of life, and yet it is the unreasoned philosophy of many. Strange how illogical we are sometimes, for nature show us changeless law. Science is only possible because nature is organized law, not chance. Why then, when it comes to human events and human existence, should we put everything in a compartment and label it "Chance and Disorder," while we are obliged to put all other things in the universe in another compartment and label it "Law and Order"? It is illogical and absurd to do so, for surely law must govern all things, human and nonhuman, great and small.

DESTINY SELF-CAUSED

The third answer to the problem of destiny is that we as immortal souls are the molders and masters of our own destiny because we started and will start all the forces which mold the circumstances in which we live. This is the point of view accepted and taught by Theosophy. It tells us that no one is to blame except ourselves for our birth conditions, our character, our opportunities, our abilities, for all these things are due to the working out of forces we have set going either in this life or in former lives. Thus all existing conditions are due either to the immediate or remote past, because, to use St. Paul's luminous simile, we are reaping the harvests which have grown from seed we have sown before: "Whatsoever a man soweth that shall he also reap."

From the seeds of good and bad actions spring the harvests of pleasant and unpleasant physical circumstances; from the seeds of attentiveness to small opportunities spring the harvests of greater opportunities; from the seeds of good and evil thoughts and desires spring the harvests of good and bad character.

These results are as inevitable as the fall of a stone to earth after it has been thrown into the air. We are what we are because of our past actions, desires and thoughts. There is no favoritism in nature; we must earn what we receive. If this idea is once grasped, then envy and resentment become impossible and we cease uselessly cursing fate.

DESTINY AND GOD

This conception of destiny does not eliminate God from the world; our idea of divinity becomes far grander than before. Instead, however, of a world so imperfectly conceived that he must constantly interfere to set things straight, we realize that the universe, even to the slightest detail, is perfect in its working because guided by exquisitely balanced natural and moral laws. When these laws are transgressed, suffering comes; when they are obeyed, happiness is ours. Because of this it is possible for us to learn right from wrong.

THE LAWS OF NATURE

Sometimes people exclaim, when they have only partially grasped this conception of destiny: "But why
should these merciless laws of destiny make us suffer
for things we have forgotten?" As this natural question
contains several misconceptions, it will be necessary to
analyze it carefully in order to gain a clear understanding of what it implies.

In the first place, what do we mean by a "law of nature"? Certainly not laws *in any sense* resembling those
turned out each year by hundreds of our legislative
bodies. A law of nature is merely a condition, an inevitable sequence. If a certain thing is done, such will be
the result, and the result never changes. Inevitableness
is the chief characteristic of natural law. Under the
same conditions of atmospheric pressure, heat *always*
causes water to boil at a certain temperature. If it were
not for the inevitable character of natural law, science
would be impossible, and because we could never
know what to expect, the wheels of industry would
cease to move. May not this same inevitableness apply
likewise to moral laws? If so, it is obvious, that if in a
past life or lives certain causes are started, they must
produce their inevitable effects, whether our *physical*
consciousness remembers the causes or not.

We should not forget that the soul always remembers, and when in our brain consciousness we are
writhing under a sense of injustice because of some
event which has happened, the soul itself is comparing
the present result with its past cause and is learning a
lesson thereby. Physical forgetfulness of the past,
therefore, should not logically be able to affect the
working of a moral law. If we have upset the equilib-
rium of nature, it must be readjusted.

MODIFICATION OF DESTINY

It is always possible, however, to neutralize a force by directing against it another force, equal in power and moving in an opposite direction. Thus if we have made mistakes in the past, we can to a considerable extent modify the results by setting in operation neutralizing forces. If we send out a strong thought of love immediately after we have made the mistake of thinking a thought of hate, we can overcome what otherwise would have been the inevitable effect of the hate. *This great possibility of modifying destiny should not be overlooked.*

Is it right to speak of any law of nature as merciless? Do we call gravity merciless, because one day, while walking along a river bank, the soil gave way under our feet and gravity dragged us to the rocks below? Of course we do not, because we realize that if gravity ceased but for a single instant, there would be a terrific explosion and this earth would drift off through space as a mere cloud of impalpable dust. Do we call nature cruel because she produces a diseased condition of our physical bodies when we become dissipated and neglect our health? Then why should we do so if the result of some similar lack of self-control, for one reason or another, *does not come at once but is postponed until a future life?* Are we not the same souls and retain full memories of all past lives, which, after all, are only days in our greater soul life?

Nature is most wise in enabling us *physically* to forget the past and start with a clean record. How many have wished and prayed for that very boon in this life! Memories are frequently a handicap and even a torment when accompanied by remorse. It is for this reason, among others, that we start afresh each life on earth. Furthermore, full memories of all our past lives would make it possible, to a considerable extent, to anticipate the future, because we could pick out the causes that would produce coming events. Now recall some month or year which was filled with sorrow and difficulty. Would we have had the courage to face that period had we known what was coming? Our very ignorance of the future was an enormous advantage, and because we did not see the events until they were actually upon us, we were victorious over them in the end. Knowledge of the future, at our present stage of evolution, would be a curse and not a help and the cause of countless failures, where ignorance of what is to be brings success.

What we do bring with us in a new incarnation, however, is the essence of our past experiences in the form in innate faculties and the voice of conscience. Whenever in business an old set of account books is closed and a new set opened, only the balances are brought forward. So when we commence a new incarnation we bring the *summation* of our past experiences in a form most suited to the needs and emergencies of physical life; hence those qualities of character, those powers to achieve, those inborn faculties which make one child different from another.

FATALISM

Self-created destiny, often mentioned in theosophical literature as "karma," is not fatalistic in the slightest. Fatalism always implies that we are bound on an iron wheel of circumstances from which no effort of our own can free us. Karma, on the contrary, says that while in truth we are bound by what we have done in the past, yet each moment we live we are molding and modifying the future by the decisions and choices we make.

Free will certainly does not mean that we are free to change the conditions of nature in any way that our whims may dictate, but that we are free to choose what we shall do *within* those conditions. If each one of us had the power to modify the world according to our several fancies, what an inconceivable chaos would result!

One of the conditions of nature is that, once we choose, we must abide by the results of our choice. In this way we learn wisdom. If we decide to jump off a wall, it does not stop our fall for one instant to wish halfway down that we were on the top again. If we jump off we must strike bottom—a cause is always followed by its effect. If we are wise we think before we jump.

PHILOSOPHY OF OPTIMISM

This conception of destiny, when once understood, results in a philosophy of optimism. Every hardship we experience is an old debt paid, and we are glad of it; instead of complaining or repining we seek eagerly for the lessons each event brings. The friends who gather round us have been our friends before; the ones we love in this life will be with us again many times in the future, for love is a tie so strong that even death cannot break it.

There is no goal too high for us to reach; if we place our goal on the heights, it may not be reached for many lives, but reach it we shall, for that which we *will* to do we can do. All that is necessary is to turn every energy in that direction, to seize every opportunity to draw nearer to it. If this is done there is no power on earth or in heaven which can prevent us from reaching it.

We may be handicapped, it is true, by foolish mistakes or contrary efforts we have made in the past, either in this life or in others, but the effects of these mistakes and efforts must in time become exhausted, and equally the new forces we are setting in operation now must produce *their* inevitable effects. So instead of bewailing our past mistakes, we resolutely set to work, under the inspiration of this philosophy, to mold the future into the likeness of our highest ideals, confident that if each moment we set going the best we know, the future, immediate and distant, will be radiant with ever-increasing happiness and filled with ever-growing opportunities. The good law may be trusted to the end.

7

THE SPLENDID GOAL

The highest conceptions of the Occult Doctrine imply that the fundamental urge of the individual soul to find the Truth which is hidden within it, is an urge to find itself. Or in other words the Seeker and the Sought are really one. This paradoxical truth suggests that evolution is a cyclic process without a beginning or end. . . . In evolution of the human soul the consciousness imprisoned within the personality is progressively released from these limitations and expands, step by step, into that original unfettered state from which it had descended. It thus completes a full circle, although we are not able to see the upper part of this circle which is hidden in the darkness of the Unmanifest.

> I. K. Taimni, The Theosophist,
> Vol. 87, No. 12, Sept., 1966

7

THE SPLENDID GOAL

GOD AND THE UNIVERSE

What is the nature of that wider life for which the long process of incarnation is preparing us? Assuredly not an inactive existence in some spiritual realm where for all eternity we remain in an ecstasy of devotional contemplation. This may appeal to the mystic and the saint, who love seclusion and freedom from the contacts of the world, but to the normal man and woman of today, a future existence of wide and beneficent activity would be more attractive and more in keeping with what is apparently the purpose of our physical existence.

Does not the greatest happiness come to us now when we have successfully accomplished some good work, created something useful or beautiful or been of service to others? There is, of course, a passing pleasure in winning a prize, receiving a pleasing gift and enjoying an entertainment or trip, but such pleasure can never equal in quality or intensity the happiness that comes when we realize that we have contributed something of value to the world.

This happiness is instinctive; it is the expression in us of the universal joy in creation. We may see that joy in the very exuberance with which nature fashions whirling atom and flashing star, colored flower and rugged crag, creeping lichen and forest giant, flying moth and laboring human, painted coral and threatening cloud, insect wing and flaming nebula. Nature models whole kingdoms of living things with inexhaustible invention, lightly touching all with charm and grace, draping some in sober hues, others in maddest colors, yet all with beauty. Some are designed in terms of pure geometry, others with wild fancy, some as of lacework, others with limitless strength. As we gaze, our hearts quicken with the creative vitality of it all, and we feel the joy of its divine Inventor as he molds form after form in plastic matter, in infinite variety to express life after life in infinite complexity. We need not depreciate the love of activity, the admiration for efficiency, the worship of achievement, which are marked characteristics of the modern person. They are the first expressions in the race of a new sense of power, which in the end will lead to mastery of the physical world. From our present efforts, misguided and unbalanced as frequently they are, will arise in time true skill in action, which is one of the ways of gaining knowledge of the Divine. We ought not to regard such efforts and ideals as merely a passing phase. Rather they are long pent-up forces bursting through the crust of civilization, the result of the onward pressure of evolution.

We shall not be able to understand the profound significance of evolution so long as we think of God as separate from the universe, existing apart somewhere in space, an *external* Creator fashioning the worlds in cosmic matter. The evolution of a universe does not resemble the building of a house, because the human artisans who wield saw and hammer are not *part* of the house. But we may compare an evolving universe to a living organism for the universe is living, and as is the case with an organism, the guiding, controlling Intelligence is within, not without.

Long ago we were told that "in him we live and move and have our being," and this seems to be literally the truth. Every form, moving or unmoving, from the tiny atom beneath our feet to the farthest star, is the *manifestation* of Divinity. In affirming this we are not advocating a crude pantheism by bringing God down to the level of matter, but we are lifting matter up to God, though beyond doubt the Divine Life infinitely transcends the material universe.

We speak carelessly of matter as if it were inert and dead, but scientific experiments have indicated that it is wonderfully sensitive, platinum responding in particular to changes in temperature amounting to only 1/100,000 of one degree. Electrical experiments have also shown that a bar of steel, far from being a cold, dead mass of metal, is composed of atoms and molecules which thrill and quiver if even a warm finger is placed on the surface of the bar.

As we gaze starwards on a brilliant night and trace the sparkling swarms of mighty suns flung bannerwise across the bowl of space, the immensity of the universe awes us to silence, and we realize something of the titanic forces which must span the interstellar spaces holding each blazing star on its appointed way. Still more intense grows the feeling of reverence when it flashes upon us that many of these millions of suns must have attendant planets which bear upon their surface living humanities similar to our own. Stirred by the thought, our imagination carries us out into the depths of space, and as we look back upon the mighty universe we have just been contemplating, it has dwindled to a distant star cluster, one among millions of other clusters which float in the silent vastnesses surrounding us. Space without end, neither top nor bottom nor sides; splendid suns without number, arranged in clusters and colossal masses of clusters, each solar system the physical body of a vast Intelligence, each star cluster the form of a still mightier Consciousness, the whole but cells and organs in the body of God, the Universal Consciousness. Then we know that we must cast aside forever all our childish ideas of God as a magnified human being and strive to think of him as the Universal Life, the Limitless Consciousness, the Eternal Love, the very source and heart of all that is. "Everything that is, is God."

When we return to contemplate the Earth, nature has taken on new dignity and a deeper significance. No longer can we look indifferently at her various kingdoms—mineral, vegetable, animal, human and superhuman—for we see that each one has sprung into being because of the pressure of the Divine Life welling up *through* matter, bearing with it countless centers of consciousness, which in the human kingdom become individualized as souls. Wave after wave of this Life pushes its way up through matter, modeling it into ever more complex forms, until out of the mineral arises the vegetable, out of the vegetable the animal, out of the animal the human, out of the human the superhuman.

Every form in the universe is ceaselessly growing, passing as the centuries speed on, from immobility to freedom, from darkness to light, from ignorance to wisdom, from a less perfect to a more perfect stage. Ultimate perfection is never reached, for ultimate perfection is God, but every living thing is continually becoming more perfect and does in time reach perfection *for its stage of growth.* Thus we may think of a perfect human, but when such perfection is reached, a more glorious goal is seen ahead, and when that is won, still another is visible. Progress is infinite; therefore happiness is infinite. Though we may gain much wisdom, there is ever more wisdom for the winning. Though we may gain true love, there is ever greater love to embody, arising as love does from the heart of the Divine. Though we may gain great skill in action, even greater skill is possible, for we are being taught in a world built by the Master Worker.

Joy becomes more intense as we advance along the evolutionary path, because there is never any end to the glories unveiled to our awakening comprehension. The universe may be compared to a kaleidoscope, so dear to the heart of every child, in which scene melts into scene with ever-increasing beauty and color, until the childish eyes are aglow with delight and expectation. So also with us as we grow upwards, but in the universe the transformations are endless, God ever concealing himself with some lovelier creation. Truly it has been said that "veil after veil shall lift, but there shall be veil after veil behind." This is the zest of life, this the inspiration of progress, this the eternal mystery of the Godhead.

EVOLUTION

"Evolution" is the name given to that limited portion of the never-ceasing progress or transformation within the universe that we are able to perceive here on earth. Our understanding of evolution is often distorted, however, because that tiny portion of the process we are now witnessing is the hardest and most trying of all. It may be compared to the uninspiring scale practice which is needed before one can become a skillful musician. All great structures and achievements have their scaffolding stage during which beauty is lacking and the surroundings are unpleasant. But the edifice at first concealed by the rough timbers is later revealed in all its beauty. So with human character, which is now being built up laboriously block by block. It is often unlovely because incomplete, but there is a beauty and unlimited possibilities in every one of us, clearly visible to a Master's eye.

There seems to be no limit to the powers we may evolve when we make the effort, for our consciousness is a ray of the divine Light, and to that ray all achievements are possible in time. We may think of each soul as a lens through which the ray of universal Light is shining, so that while we are true spiritual individuals, even as an image of the one sun cast by a burning glass is separate from all other images, nevertheless we are but reflections of the one great Consciousness. Has it not been said that we were created in the image of God, and do we not recall the admonishing words: "Know ye not that ye are the Temple of God and the Spirit of God dwelleth in you?"

THE NATURE OF GROWTH

Growth is not the *addition* of qualities to our character; it is the stimulation to activity and expression of qualities we possessed all the time, but in a *latent* condition. Development is therefore unfolding of the pow-

ers which are hidden within, even as the beauty of the
rose is concealed in the bud. The purpose of evolution—with its trials and hardships, difficulties and suc-
cesses, loves and hates, pleasures and disappointments,
luxuries and privations—is to stir us, coax us and if
need be force us to awaken to activity and power the
hidden, slumbering faculties of the soul, and to show
us how we may master world after world if only we
make the effort.

Truth is within ourselves; it takes no rise
From outward things, whate'er you may believe.
. . . and to *know*,
Rather consists in opening out a way
Whence the imprisoned splendor may escape,
Than effecting entry for a light
Supposed to be without.

Robert Browning, "Paracelsus"

Most people do not learn either willingly or volun-
tarily but seek to spend their days in amusement and
fleeting pleasures. Sooner or later nature, but an as-
pect of God, finds it necessary to resort to drastic measures in order to teach them those things they must
learn. Growth is swift when we take our own evolution
in hand and strive to cooperate with the divine will
which makes for progress. But advancement is pain-
fully slow for millions of human beings because they
merely exist, mechanically following a daily routine,
and never think of seeking the purpose of life.

When we see around us men and women who can do
with ease that which we cannot do and possess greater
powers than ours—a strong character, a superb intellect, a soaring spirituality, a power to achieve that is
inspiring—there is no cause for despair, any more than

a child should become despondent because she is not yet a student in college. Such men and women have outstripped us in certain ways and are therefore nearer to the splendid goal than we, but if we put forth similar and equal efforts, we shall lift ourselves to their level. It may take years or even lives to accomplish this end, depending upon our present stage of development, but nothing can prevent us from reaching *any* level of achievement upon which we set our will.

THE SPLENDID GOAL

The splendid goal is not a changeless thing; it varies with the development of each aspiring consciousness, for it is the next step forward in evolution for that consciousness. For an intelligent animal, the splendid goal is becoming human; for a human being it is becoming a superhuman, a Master; for a Master it is a still more stupendous height far beyond our comprehension. For all it is the gleaming gateway ahead, on the other side of which open out the illumined vistas of a larger life.

INITIATION

Initiation is the indescribable *welcoming* by the Masters, the elders of the race, of those men and women who, through varied experience gained during many lives on earth, have risen to that level of development where they are nearing the point of graduation from the world-school. Initiation is the goal for every human being, and though for millions its attainment is still remote, many are coming into incarnation now for whom initiation is comparatively near at hand. A very few will gain it in this life if they were so fortunate as to commence their training while still young; a number will win their way to this superb height next life on earth if they take their evolution in hand *now;* many, however, will reach this glorious consummation of physical existence in only a few incarnations if they commence to practice steadfastly in *this life* on earth those simple rules of physical, moral, mental and spiritual education so clearly explained in Theosophy.*

To reach initiation the help of a Master is needed, for there are many lessons to be learned and much training to undergo, both in this and in the invisible worlds. Therefore one must know something of the Masters, of their work for humanity and how their attention may be attracted so that we may receive the necessary assistance.

When a person through the long course of evolution, reaches perfection as a human being and is therefore under no obligation or necessity to reincarnate any longer, he or she does not withdraw into the utter bliss of some spiritual realm, leaving us younger brothers to struggle unaided with our many sorrows, trials and problems. Unselfishness and compassion are two of the many priceless lessons thoroughly taught in this world-school, and all who graduate from it are embodiments of these two spiritual qualities. Therefore, one who has completed human evolution, unless assigned to other work in the solar system for which there is need, remains in the invisible worlds surrounding the earth and, in a most powerful way, assists in the evolution of humanity.

---

*Those who are really in earnest cannot do better than to obtain a copy of *At the Feet of the Master* and strive to make part of their character the precepts so simply laid down in that wonderful little book of the higher life.

THE WORK OF THE MASTERS

Those who have thus remained are often spoken of as "Masters" (though in a stricter sense the title "Master" is restricted to those of the perfected ones who accept pupils), and they form collectively the Great White Lodge or Occult Hierarchy, traditions of which have existed for centuries in the Orient. The evolution of the whole of humanity takes place under the guiding care of this mighty spiritual organization, and in countless ways the individual Masters help not only the race as a whole, but also individual men and women when they are found worthy.

Though many of the Masters are in incarnation physically, they live in seclusion and seldom mingle in the hurry and rush of civilization. It would be a useless expenditure of energy for them to take part in our physical activities, as their beneficent work is done almost wholly and to much better advantage in the invisible worlds. There they can come more intimately in contact with the many millions of souls who populate this planet and are able to help them more effectively than would be possible while moving among us physically, for here we are handicapped decidedly by the limitations of the brain and accordingly are much less responsive to spiritual forces.

The Masters, from time to time when civilization is ready, introduce new ideals and aspirations into human minds by sending powerful waves of thought and feeling into the mental currents of the subtler worlds. These flood the higher levels of the emotional and mental worlds and are caught up and repeated physically by receptive people. It is for this reason that stimulating ideals, forceful ideas, important inventions and higher moral standards so often arise spontaneously in many parts of the world about the same time. The cause of these sudden enthusiasms—as, for example, the intense desire for universal peace, the radiant ideal of religious tolerance, the inspiring dream of a cooperative civilization, the sense of personal responsibility for the welfare of others, the quickening feeling of the need for universal brotherhood—will forever remain an enigma, until we learn of this hidden labor of our divine Teachers.

Rarely one of the Masters comes out openly into the world in order to give, with the skill possible only to a Master, some important truth or teaching, or to help with his physical presence in the molding of civilization in some new and urgent way. More often the Masters send pupils into the world to influence civilization in some necessary direction, either by their skill in leadership, genius in art, wisdom in writing or eloquence in speaking. The world is led from ideal to ideal, from height to height, largely by the influence of great personalities. If we had the power to look behind the scenes, we should find that many of the great men and women of history, both immediate and remote, were the conscious or unconscious messengers of the Masters.

Sometimes the Masters find it necessary to establish a movement or organization, through which they can more adequately and widely convey certain points of view which must be generally accepted before civilization can take its next step forward. It was for this purpose that the Theosophical Society came into existence as a small though definite part of the great plan for the helping of humanity—even as other movements have their part to play in this plan. One of the important reasons, among others, for which the Society exists is to influence public opinion to accept a number of stimulating spiritual ideals, helpful philosophical truths, fundamental interpretations of life and destiny and wholesome information regarding unseen things, in order that humanity may have an *adequate* working philosophy of life during the important changes in the established order which are now taking place. Theosophical information has been of value in turning back the rising tide of materialism which threatened, in the late nineteenth century, to engulf all spiritual aspiration, and it has also helped to restore the power to inspire and purify to some of the great religions of the world—Christianity, Hinduism, Buddhism and Zoroastrianism. Although Theosophy in its purity, is unknown to most—because their ideas concerning it have been based not upon study but upon prejudiced rumors and the distorted opinions of others—nevertheless its unlabeled teachings have spread everywhere, and many of the liberal and progressive ideas now generally accepted were considered peculiar to Theosophy in its early years. It is by this slow absorption of new ideas that civilization advances.

If the Masters exist and are guiding civilization, we may wonder why so much crime, injustice and ignorance exist. We should realize, however, that the Masters never coerce the world or try to *force* humanity along any line of progress, however desirable. They help in their powerful way whenever the slightest opportunity is offered, and they constantly encourage and stimulate, but they never compel. If they had bent our wills to theirs, this civilization would be far more perfect than it is now. But we would still be only obedient children instead of developing, as we have partially done, the strength and initiative of self-reliance. Lessons taught by precept alone are never so deeply rooted as those impressed upon us by actual experience, and hence it is that the Masters have allowed us to experiment and thereby test our imperfect ideas, realizing that only in this slow way—the way of evolution—can wisdom most surely be gained. Mistakes, failures and follies are more effective teachers than good counsel and advice.

The aim of the Masters is to evolve a civilization which may be relied upon to do what is right at any cost, not because of precepts obediently followed, but because of clear-sighted wisdom won in many a losing battle against wrong, oppression and injustice. They desire for the race to be pure, not because of the un-tested virtue of innocence, but because it has arisen from the foulness of vice cleansed and made wise by inevitable suffering. They plan for humanity to be wholly brotherly, not because of ignorance of hate, but because we have learned through experiencing enmity, selfishness and competition that there is nothing so priceless as love, and that not one thing can be of last-ing benefit to individuals or nations if it has been gained at the expense of others.

THE POWER OF CONTRASTS

We learn only by contrasts; right is seen by contrast with wrong, purity by contrast with impurity, strength by contrast with weakness. This knowledge is the gift of physical experience, through which alone such con-trasts are possible, and gaining it is worth everything through which we must go in our many incarnations. Experience is the magic wand that awakens the spiri-tual seed of consciousness after it has been planted in matter.

We may imagine some ideal civilization springing forth full-formed from the Divine Mind, which would be wonderful, glorious beyond all telling. But it would be composed of a humanity of beautiful dolls, obeying blindly the will of their Designer, and not a civilization which, though less beautiful, is infinitely more inspiring because formed of spiritual intelligences who have won their way to their present standing by sheer mastery of circumstances, and, as scarred veterans, command homage and admiration. In this thought may lie hidden the inner necessity, not only for physical existence, but for the manifestation of the universe.

We should not shrink from experience, even though hard, for experience alone can help us win the splendid goal. *Knowledge of the world is as necessary to evolving humanity as is spiritual understanding,* and we eventually shall gain both. For most of us, the swiftest growth comes when we labor diligently in the world, striving to solve the problems, overcome the difficulties and manage the situations of daily life with efficiency and high motives. Some think of the world as spread with the snares of a devil and counsel turning our thoughts constantly to heaven; Theosophy regards the world as the crucible of God in the white heat of which character is refined. Others believe that spiritual progress is impossible in the midst of worldly life and advise retirement from the world; Theosophy states that the instruction we receive in daily life is absolutely necessary here and hereafter, for without the detailed knowledge and wide experience which physical existence alone can give us, we shall not be able to accomplish successfully or even commence the mighty work in the unseen realms for which these many incarnations on earth have been fitting us.

MEETING EXPERIENCE

There are certain ways of *meeting* experience that are most effective in their results, for not only do they intensify life to a remarkable extent, give richness and meaning to every event and make us attentive to opportunities, but they also hasten our development, and above all bring us forcibly to the attention of one of the Masters. These attitudes, which we should seek to cultivate as we go forth to meet experience, are as follows:

TEACHABLENESS

So many people go through life complaining of the hardships of their lot, anticipating troubles which never come, blaming others for their own failures, fretful over small things and remarks, fussing with trivialities. It is refreshing to meet someone who thoughtfully examines each experience, pleasant or unpleasant, sees its lesson, notes where he or she has been at fault and quietly determines not to make the same mistake again. There is so much subtle egotism in most of us that rarely do we think of ourselves as the cause of many of our troubles. Practically everyone is convinced, when something unpleasant has happened, that someone else is to blame. But when anything particularly fortunate occurs, we are usually willing to acknowledge—modestly, of course—our responsibility in the matter. Considerable development is shown when one is willing to acknowledge responsibility for failure.

Every teacher will recall the pleasure felt when a pupil eagerly cooperated in learning the lessons assigned, but probably remembers also with equal vividness the discouragement when it was necessary to force a lesson on a stubborn child who, careless and indifferent, persisted in idling away his time. In this world-school many of us resemble such foolish children, and no doubt that is one of the reasons why Mother Nature is obliged to administer a punishment now and then, in the form of strenuous experience, to make us learn.

Far greater happiness would be ours if, instead of thoughtlessly letting the days slip by, we sought for the priceless lessons they bring. Nothing happens by chance; there is a purpose, and an excellent purpose, in all things and events. Our business is to find that purpose and profit by it; if we do not, the experience is repeated again and again, with minor variations, until we do.

We often make ourselves miserable by clinging too tenaciously to our possessions and associations. "Transplanting is as good for us as for seedlings," tersely says Annie Besant. The chief value of the attractive things of the world is that they call forth efforts in us to gain them, and efforts awaken the power to achieve. Possessions are of about as much intrinsic value to us, who are deathless souls, as text-books and a notebook are to a schoolboy. When they have accomplished their purpose, there is no reason why they should not be discarded. The soul cannot use possessions in its own world where consciousness is the one reality, and so when on earth those things we have gathered together are taken away from us, it is wiser to turn bright-eyed to whatever else nature has in store than to complain, grieve and get angry, like children deprived of their toys. Though we can realize physically but little of the richer, fuller life of our soul consciousness in the heaven-world, our duty is to be keenly alert to the meaning and purpose of everything that happens, in order that the soul within may gain clear pictures of the world without and in time master the complexities of physical existence. The Masters rejoice in helping those who are willing to be taught.

EFFICIENCY

The ability to work without waste of energy, loss of movement or unnecessary friction is one of the great ideals of our modern day, and is valuable equally to the aspirant for spiritual advancement as to the business person. Efficiency implies concentration, paying close attention to everything we do; it is a faculty of much value as it stimulates a magnificent mental development. If we are practicing efficiency, nothing should be done carelessly or hastily but everything with full attention, each action preceded by thought and guided by judgment. Efficiency has no place for slipshod methods or slovenly workmanship; whatever is done,— whether sweeping a room or managing a factory, inscribing a letter or writing a book—should be done with all our might and all our skill. We should also be willing to profit by the experiences of others and therefore make a point of reading carefully the best which has been written upon a subject before we act or judge. How many mistakes and false opinions would be eliminated if this rule were followed! Those who seek the Masters would do well to practice efficiency in all things.

COURAGE

Those who take their evolution in hand need courage, for destiny responds to their appeal for progress, and the current of life moves on more swiftly. Many difficulties will confront us, arising out of mistakes and wrong judgments we have made in the past, and frequently we shall falter and fail, for we are but human. Failure in itself means little, however, if we have the courage to go on again after every setback, wringing from each failure its drop of wisdom. We must have high courage to play the game of life well and with spirit, as becomes strong souls, and never to fear the future, no matter what it may bring.

When we realize that our destiny is actually self-caused and that the sequence or arrangement of the chief events that come into our lives is in the charge of omniscient Intelligences, we cast aside all apprehension and go bravely forward with heads erect, knowing that nothing can harm the inner Self. All our destiny can do is deprive us of our little possessions, cause us some temporary sufferings, or strike away our physical body. Through it all *we* pass unscathed, and if we have knowledge, unshaken, for in us flames the divine fire.

Our destiny is so wisely adjusted that nothing ever comes which is too much to bear, *if we keep up courage*. Many a person has been overwhelmed physically and gone down to apparent defeat, only to rise triumphant and rejoicing on the other side of death, because of a debt well paid and a victory won. No matter how hard the battle goes, fight on, and above all never make the mistake of thinking that suicide will make things easier and bring forgetfulness. We may kill the physical body, but we cannot annihilate memory or remorse, and those who have slain their bodies when courage failed found life even harder on the other side. Never give up, struggle on, even against heavy odds, for the spirit within is indestructible and imperishable and knows not defeat.

BROTHERLINESS

Many people, responding to the call of brotherhood, have started out bravely to be of service to their fellows but, meeting with ingratitude, indifference and misunderstanding, have become discouraged, disheartened and even bitter. Whereupon they let the world go on unaided, declaring that brotherly service was an impossible ideal. Such experience is almost inevitable at this stage of evolution, as all who serve will testify, because humanity is undeveloped in so many ways. But does not this very absence of responsive feeling on the part of those we seek to help tell us, more plainly than before, that service is needed? Ingratitude would only inspire more earnest efforts on our part if our attitude were right.

The difficulty is that while we believe ourselves to be wholly unselfish in our desire to serve, yet a taint of selfishness has crept in, for all unconsciously we crave praise, recognition, gratitude and even applause. Not receiving these, we feel hurt and disappointed. If we were absolutely unselfish, we would not ask for thanks but labor for the sake of the work and because we love our fellow human beings.

Love is the essence of brotherliness, and unless we feel true affection for those about us, with all their faults and weaknesses, our efforts to serve will not long endure. There are too many disappointments. But when we love, it inspires us with that steady enthusiasm, emotional or mental according to our temperament, which we call devotion, and with devotion a person even with few talents, may be of great service to the world and go far toward the Masters. To such people no service is too small, no labor too arduous. They think of all around them as brothers and sisters, and that is enough. It is not without deep meaning that Masters prefer Brothers above all other titles, and that those who have reached this lofty height never even think of receiving praise or recognition, because their service of humanity is perfect and therefore utterly selfless. The Masters are joyous beyond all telling because they never think of themselves but ever of the happiness of others. Should we not go and do likewise?

In this marvelous world-school, everyone possibly strong enough to become a leader is tested, as an important piece of machinery is tested in an engineering laboratory. If the tests, which are those of daily life, are passed successfully, wider opportunities arise, but if they are not passed the candidate for leadership is placed among the followers again for further instruction. Every day we see people rise above their fellows only to fall back once more into obscurity; they were not strong enough nor big enough to wield power. As Elbert Hubbard said: "The man who is worthy of being a leader of men will never complain of the stupidity of his helpers, of the ingratitude of mankind, or of the inappreciation of the public. These things are all a part of the great game of life, and to meet them and not go down before them in discouragement and defeat, is the final proof of power."

DISCRIMINATION

There is a sense of values called "discrimination," which when developed enables us to choose correctly between right and wrong, truth and falsehood, the real and the unreal, the important and the unimportant. Though of the utmost significance, discrimination cannot be taught by precept, rule or book; experience alone can awaken this godlike faculty. Because of the infinite varieties of experience, no two sets of conditions between which we must choose are ever exactly alike; hence rules are useless and we must rely upon whatever judgment we possess.

Our power to discriminate measures exactly our position on the evolutionary pathway, and unerring discrimination is found only in a Master, because such a one has completed human evolution. We may do much, however, to improve the accuracy of our decisions, and thereby awaken discrimination, by striving each time we choose to do what is brotherly, what is pure, what is thoughtful, taking always into consideration the needs of others rather than our own desires. Discrimination should be used especially in deciding where we can best be of service, for many people attempt that for which they are not fitted and thrust themselves where they have no business. Intrusion does not constitute service.

Does this life in which we strive to be teachable, efficient, courageous, brotherly and discriminative seem too difficult, the goal too high? It will not seem so if once we feel the power and urge of the soul within. But to feel the prompting of that greater spiritual Self, we must calm the mind and emotions until our subtle bodies are as still as the unruffled surface of a mountain lake. Then the light and peace of the soul flood the mind and brain and we know ourselves to be divine. The soul is a shadowy unreality to most people, because they are ceaselessly engaged with external things and have never tried to sense that spiritual Presence, the "unknown guest," who awaits so silently just beyond the reach of our ever-active, useful little minds until we bid it enter and assume command as *At the Feet of the Master* puts it: "When your body wishes something, stop and think whether *you* really wish it. For *you* are God, and you will only what God wills; but you must dig deep down into yourself to find the God within you, and listen to His voice, which is *your* voice."

REACHING THE MASTER

If we yearn to find the Masters but hesitate to try because of our many imperfections, we should realize that they never ask the impossible but always allow for

our mistakes and failings, for they have not forgotten
that long ago they too were as frail as we. Truly they
have been called the Masters of Wisdom and Compassion, and we may trust them utterly, for their great
love and guiding care is divine in its splendor and
power.

Words alone do not attract their attention; they
judge our fitness for special assistance by our deeds
and not by our appeals, however eloquent. Social
standing does not help us, blue blood is of no avail,
wealth and possessions cannot assist, for the Masters do
not judge by the standards of the world. Our advancement depends entirely upon our character, our self-
mastery, the use to which we have put our talents. If
we have used our faculties for selfish gain and pleasure,
if our thoughts are unregulated and our emotions impure, obviously we are not yet ready for the Master.
But if we have used our talents for the benefit of others
and have at least partially succeeded in controlling our
thoughts and refining our emotions, then the Master
knows us in the invisible worlds, though we may not as
yet know him. If we are in earnest, our next step is to
learn all we can about the Path, as it is called in Theosophy, and deliberately to commence and steadily
continue that training of mind, emotions and body so
necessary to success.

Sometimes people believe that they can serve humanity only by giving up all family ties, business obligations and duties and devoting themselves entirely to
altruistic and other benevolent work. If we are *free* to
do such work, we of course have cause for rejoicing,
but if we have already taken upon ourselves duties and
obligations, these responsibilities come first in the eyes
of the Masters. To shirk one's responsibilities is always
a blunder, and if we do so in order to serve, such ser-

vice does not lead us to the splendid goal. A Master
spoke these words to one who followed him, as re-
corded in *At the Feet of the Master:* "Because you try
to take up higher work, you must not forget your ordinary duties, for until they are done you are not free for
other service. You should undertake no new worldly
duties; but those which you have already taken upon
you, you must perfectly fulfill—all clear and reasonable
duties which you yourself recognize, that is, not imag-
inary duties which others try to impose upon you."

All good work becomes service when done for the
sake of others; it does not matter whether that work
lies in a business office, in a school, in a factory or in a
home. It is not what we do that constitutes service; it is
why we do it—for self or for others. Unselfishness and
forgetfulness of self are priceless qualifications in the
higher life.

In exact proportion to our ability to help, encourage
and inspire others will be the swiftness of our approach
to initiation, and those who are wise train themselves
carefully along some special line of service—teaching,
writing, speaking, artistic power, or skill in some useful
way—so that they may go to the Master, when they ask
his assistance, bearing in their hands some gift of value
as did the wise men of old. The Masters do not need
incense and gold, but they do prize our offerings of
service to humanity, for they have dedicated the whole
of their mighty powers to service, and if we would
reach them and share in their joy, we must follow in
their footsteps, and as apprentices, strive to become
like them. Great shall be our happiness if we lay the
gifts of a trained mind, pure emotions and skilled
hands upon the altar of service, and in the midst of
daily life bring the calm strength, the sweet serenity,
the radiant joyousness of spiritual consecration.

FOR FURTHER READING

C. W. Leadbeater, *The Hidden Side of Things.*
Discusses the unseen worlds around us and how they influence us. Cooper drew heavily on such clairvoyant investigations, by C. W. Leadbeater and others, for his *Theosophy Simplified.*
————. *Man Visible and Invisible.*
Leadbeater described his clairvoyant impressions of the auras of different people to an artist, who painted the pictures that appear in this book under his direction.
————. *The Masters and the Path.*
An impression of the Masters, their ideals, and their methods of training disciples.
Annie Besant. *From the Outer Court to the Inner Sanctum.*
A talk that gives an inspiring account of the spiritual life, by a former President of the Theosophical Society who was a distinguished speaker in the style of her day.
————. *Karma.*
A description of different kinds of karma and the ways that we interact with them.
————. *Seven Principles of Man.*
A clear discussion of the complexities of the human constitution, with its various principles such as the physical body, the emotions, two aspects of the mind, intuition, etc.
John Algeo, *Reincarnation Explored.*
A contemporary look at the pros and cons of reincarnation and what it means in our lives.
H. P. Blavatsky, *Key to Theosophy* (abridged by Joy Mills).
The primary teacher of Theosophical philosophy and a

founder of the Theosophical movement answers questions about life after death, karma, the human constitution, etc. Robert Ellwood, *Theosophy: A Modern Expression of the Wisdom of the Ages.* A contemporary overview of Theosophy that is readable yet somewhat in depth.

Shirley Nicholson, *Ancient Wisdom—Modern Insight.* Some basic principles of Theosophy presented by H. P. Blavatsky in her source book of esoteric philosophy, *The Secret Doctrine,* as corroborated by developments in modern thought.

INDEX

QUEST BOOKS
are published by
The Theosophical Society in America,
Wheaton, Illinois 60189-0270,
a branch of a world organization
dedicated to the promotion of the unity of
humanity and the encouragement of the study of
religion, philosophy, and science, to the end that
we may better understand ourselves and our place in
the universe. The Society stands for complete
freedom of individual search and belief.
In the Classics Series well-known
theosophical works are made
available in popular editions.
For more information
write or call.
1-312-668-1571

Additional books on the theosophical philosophy

ABRIDGEMENT OF THE SECRET DOCTRINE—
H. P. Blavatsky. Ed. by E. Preston & C. Humphreys

ANCIENT WISDOM—Annie Besant

ANCIENT WISDOM: MODERN INSIGHT—
Shirley Nicholson

BASIC IDEAS OF OCCULT WISDOM—
Anna Kennedy Winner

DIVINE PLAN—Geoffrey Barborka

EXPLORING THE GREAT BEYOND —Geoffrey Farthing

'I' THE STORY OF THE SELF—Michal J. Eastcott

KEY TO THEOSOPHY—H. P. Blavatsky

MAHATMA LETTERS TO A. P. SINNETT—
Compiled by Trevor A. Barker

MAN, GOD AND THE UNIVERSE—I. K. Taimni

MASTERS AND MEN —Virginia Hanson

QUESTIONS ON OCCULTISM—Ernest Wood

SECRET DOCTRINE—Helena Petrovna Blavatsky

SPACE TIME AND SELF—E. Norman Pearson

These titles are available from:
QUEST BOOKS
306 West Geneva Road
Wheaton, Illinois 60187